THE HUMMINGBIRD BOOK

What heavenly tints in mingling radiance fly!

Each rapid movement gives a different dye;

Like scales of burnished gold they dazzling show —

Now sink to shade, now like a furnace glow!

Alexander Wilson, 1776–1813
Early American Ornithologist

Also by Donald and Lillian Stokes

THE BIRD FEEDER BOOK

AND
Stokes Nature Guides,
which include:

A Guide to Nature in Winter
A Guide to Bird Behavior, Volume I
A Guide to Bird Behavior, Volume II
A Guide to Bird Behavior, Volume III
A Guide to Observing Insect Lives
A Guide to Enjoying Wildflowers
A Guide to Animal Tracking and Behavior

Also by Donald Stokes

The Natural History of Wild Shrubs and Vines

THE HUMMINGBIRD BOOK

THE COMPLETE GUIDE TO ATTRACTING, IDENTIFYING, AND ENJOYING HUMMINGBIRDS

Donald and Lillian Stokes

Authors of *Stokes Nature Guides*

Illustrations and range maps
by Donald Stokes

LITTLE, BROWN AND COMPANY

Boston Toronto London

FIRST EDITION

Photograph Acknowledgments

Animals/Animals: E. R. Degginger—28; Marcia Griffen—23.
Aspects, Inc.: 88
Willard Colburn: 53
Bruce Coleman, Inc: Bob and Clara Calhoun—7, 9, 27 top, 30, 41, 45, 49, 51, 57, 59, 61, 63, 65, 69, 79; John S. Dunning—86; Kenneth Fink—77; Wayne Lankinen—vi, 1, 25, 73.
David Collister—80.
Cornell Laboratory of Ornithology: Brian Daw—67; I. Jeklin—71; Patricia Meacham—46; W. A. Paff—87.
Maslowski Photo: 13, 14, 16 bottom, 19, 21, 31, 32, 33, 74, 75.
Theron McCuen: 84.
Tim Morse, Morse Photography: 3, 5, 12.
Opus: 8.
Penn Pak, Inc.: 89.
Photo Researchers: Gilbert Grant—43; Anthony Mercieca—10.
Sid Rucker: i, 4, 11, 16 top, 29, 37, 55, 81, 82, 83, 85.
Stokes Nature Company: 18, 24.
VIREO: H. Brokaw—35; H. Cruickshank—15 bottom; S. LaFrance—17 bottom; D. and M. Zimmerman—15 top, 17 top.

Library of Congress Cataloging-in-Publication Data

Stokes, Don
     The hummingbird book : the complete guide to attracting, identifying, and enjoying hummingbirds / Don and Lillian Stokes
          p. cm.
     ISBN 0-316-81715-5
     1. Hummingbirds. 2. Birds, Attracting of. I. Stokes, Lillian
II. Title
QL696.A558S76 1989
598.8'99—dc20   89–31648
                                                                                    CIP

10 9 8 7 6 5

Designed by Donald and Lillian Stokes

RRD OH

*Published simultaneously in Canada
by Little, Brown & Company (Canada) Limited*

PRINTED IN THE UNITED STATES OF AMERICA

CONTENTS

A male ruby-throated hummingbird,
taking nectar from wild columbine.

ENJOYING HUMMINGBIRDS

We will never forget our first look at a hummingbird, many years ago. We had dutifully planted our property with the flowers we knew hummingbirds liked and had hung up hummingbird feeders, but no hummingbirds had arrived. After several months of waiting, we were just about to give up when one day we went to the garden to admire the first bloom of the cardinal flower.

Suddenly, a flash of iridescence caught our eye and "poof," a female ruby-throated hummingbird hovered right before us. It reminded us of that famous pixie, Tinker Bell, from the story of Peter Pan, and for a moment we expected a sprinkling of pixie dust to float down upon us.

From that magic day on, hummingbirds have been a part of our lives and have enchanted us every spring through every fall. Whenever we watch them our minds leave our human concerns, and we experience a renewed sense of wonder and appreciation for the living things around us.

We have written this book for you, so that you too might bring the magic of hummingbirds into your life.

It is not hard to attract hummingbirds almost anywhere in the United States and southern Canada if you create favorable habitats and put up hummingbird feeders. We will show you how to do this and will explain how to identify hummingbirds and how to photograph hummingbirds. Then we will reveal all the fascinating features of hummingbird behavior that you can watch for and that will expand your feeling of amazement about these tiniest birds.

So start today. Use this guide to attract and enjoy hummingbirds. We guarantee your life will be the richer for it.

We wish you good luck and Happy Hummingbirding!

Don and Lillian Stokes

A female ruby-throated hummingbird hovering.

HUMMINGBIRD FEEDERS

One of the best ways to attract hummingbirds and thus have the enjoyment of watching them in your yard is to buy a hummingbird feeder, fill it with a sugar-water solution, and place it in your garden. Putting it near flowers to which hummingbirds may be drawn will make it even more attractive.

Commercial Feeders

There are many fine commercial hummingbird feeders now on the market, with new ones appearing all the time. Most of these feeders have flower patterns or red parts on them so that they are attractive to hummingbirds.

There are basically two designs. One type consists of an inverted bottle that empties into a lower reservoir with feeding holes. The vacuum created at the top of the bottle is what keeps the liquid from draining out. The simplest form of this type of feeder is a small inverted bottle with a rubber stopper and glass tube coming out the bottom.

The other type of feeder is simply a container with holes in its cover through which the hummers reach to get the fluid. Many of these are thin disks with representations of flowers on the upper surface. You may want to experiment with different models of feeders to find which ones work best for you.

How to Choose

When choosing a feeder, look at it carefully. Ask the store attendant if you can take it apart, for this is essential to cleaning it out. You will be doing lots of filling and cleaning of the feeder, so make sure you can reach all areas to scrub them thoroughly. (People use bottle brushes and pipe cleaners to make this job easier.)

Start with smaller feeders and wait until your hummingbird customers are regularly emptying these before going for the larger sizes. This will ensure that your feeder solution will not sit too long in the feeder and spoil. If someone gives you a larger-size feeder as a gift, remember that you do not have to fill it all the way up; just put in the amount of solution that the hummingbirds will consume in a day or two.

There are feeders made out of plastic or glass or a combination of the two. There are pros and cons to the use of each material. Plastic doesn't break, but, on the other hand, some people feel that glass is easier to clean. There are many quality feeders on the market made out of each material.

To Perch or Not to Perch

Perches are a useful, although not essential, feature on hummingbird feeders. If the feeder has perches, the hummers will use them. If it doesn't, the hummers will happily hover at the feeding holes, just the way they do when drinking from flowers in the wild. When they want to perch they will go to a nearby shrub or tree. Hummingbirds take frequent breaks from their energy-intensive hovering flight; one study found that they spend over 60 percent of their time perched. One potential problem with perches: larger birds, such as orioles, may use the perches to get at the sugar water and exclude the hummingbirds. You can get around this problem by temporarily removing the perches or adding feeders without perches.

Where to Put the Feeder

The best place to put feeders initially is near flowers that are attractive to hummingbirds.

Some hummingbird feeders made by (from left to right): 1. Aspects, Inc., 2. North States Industries, Inc., 3. Heath Manufacturing Co., 4. Opus, 5. Droll Yankees, Inc., 6. Presto Galaxy, Inc. For addresses of manufacturers see Resources, pages 88–89.

Or, even better, where hummingbirds have been seen feeding. It is preferable to have already created a habitat where hummingbirds are likely to visit. For how to do this, see the chapter "Hummingbird Gardening," pages 24–27.

Try to place the feeders where they will be protected from the wind and where there is some shade. Wind jostles the feeder and may make the sugar solution spill, and hot sun shining all day on the feeder can cause the sugar solution to spoil more quickly.

Feeders may be suspended from a wire or string and hung from a limb, garden stake, or other support. Several companies make special metal supports intended just for hanging hummingbird feeders in your garden. Other feeders are made to be window mounted with suction cups for close-up views of the hummingbirds.

How Many Feeders?

Once you have attracted hummingbirds, the feeder will become a source of constant entertainment as the hummingbirds zoom in and out and chase one another, jockeying for position to feed. Hummingbirds can be very aggressive around sources of food and will try to keep other hummers away. A pecking order may form among the hummers at the feeder with some birds or species being dominant over others.

To reduce the competition and allow more hummers to feed, try putting up a second, third, or even more feeders.

On our property when one female ruby-throat started to monopolize the feeder, we placed a second feeder on the other side of our house, out of her view. Soon, a second hummingbird started using this feeder, always approaching it from the woods adjacent to our house, possibly to keep from being seen and chased by the female.

Homemade Feeders

While the majority of people use commercial feeders, some people begin feeding hummingbirds by making their own feeders. They use small pill vials, test tubes, or small jars, and paint them red so that they resemble a red flower. Then they attach the vials to garden stakes, or hang them from other supports. Water bottles sold in pet stores for guinea pigs or caged birds are also used by people as hummingbird feeders, usually with decorations like red ribbons added to attract the hummers.

Black-chinned hummingbird at a feeder made by Perky-Pet Products, Inc.

Some hummingbird feeders made by (from left to right): 1. Briggs Associates Inc., 2. Perky-Pet Products, Inc., 3. Rubbermaid, Inc., 4. Hyde Bird Feeder Co., 5. Penn Pak, Inc. For addresses of manufacturers see Resources, pages 88–89.

SUGAR SOLUTIONS

After getting a hummingbird feeder, the next step is to fill it! You have two choices at this point: you can either buy one of the commercial mixtures or you can make your own solution.

Homemade Mixtures

Here is a recipe for making your own mixture.

Recipe for Homemade Mixture:

1 part sugar (not honey)

4 parts water

Boil for 1 to 2 minutes. Cool.

Store extra in refrigerator.

Why is this mixture attractive to hummingbirds? Table sugar is essentially a kind of sugar called sucrose. Although flower nectar contains 3 types of sugar — sucrose, glucose, and fructose — it is mostly sucrose. Taste-test experiments with Anna's, black-chinned, and rufous hummingbirds revealed that sucrose was preferred over the other types of sugars.

A Sweet Tooth

The concentration of the sugar is also important. We recommend a 1 to 4 ratio of sugar to water because it approximates the ratio of sugar to water found in the nectar of many hummingbird flowers. A recent study of 21 native California wildflowers visited by hummingbirds showed that their nectar had an average sugar concentration of 21 percent. This is sweet enough to attract the hummers without being too sweet. If you increase the concentration of sugar, it may be harder for the birds to digest; if you decrease the concentration, they may lose interest.

Boiling the solution helps retard fermentation. Sugar-and-water solutions are subject to rapid spoiling, especially in hot weather. Do not leave sugar and water in a hummingbird feeder longer than 48 hours when the temperature is over 60 degrees.

Never Offer Honey

Do not use honey or artificial sweeteners in place of sugar when making a feeding solution. Honey ferments easily and can cause a fungus that affects hummingbirds' tongues and can be fatal to the birds. Artificial sweeteners should also be avoided for they have no food value; they do not give the birds the calories that they need.

Is Sugar Enough?

Some people worry that a sugar-and-water solution is not nutritious enough to meet hummingbirds' needs. It certainly gives them power for their incredible aerobatics, but they do need more than just sugar. Years ago, people who tried to raise hummingbirds in captivity found that the birds could not be sustained on a diet of sugar water alone. Scientists today feed hummingbirds in captivity vitamins, minerals, fruit flies, and other nutrients, as well as sugar-and-water solutions.

Wild hummingbirds likewise get their nutrition by eating many other things besides the sugar water from feeders and the nectar from flowers. Just watch them sometime! All hummingbirds eat a substantial number of small insects and spiders, gleaning them from twigs and leaves like warblers or catching them in the air like flycatchers. They also eat the tiny insects inside the flowers from which they sip nectar. Look for this feeding behavior when the birds leave your feeders.

Red Food Dye

Because the color red is so attractive to hummingbirds, many people have added red food dye to their sugar-water solutions. Also, it is said that the red color makes it easier to monitor fluid level in the feeders. Nonetheless, the use of red food dye to color sugar-water solutions has been a matter of ongoing controversy.

In 1975 the federal Food and Drug Administration took red food dye #2 off the market because there was a question about its safety for human consumption. Consequently many people are now choosing not to use any red food dye in their feeders. There is red on the hummingbird feeders anyway, and this should make them sufficiently attractive to the birds.

We spoke with a representative of the federal Food and Drug Administration who said that all the red dyes on the market now have been extensively studied and approved as safe for human and animal consumption, although no specific tests have been done with birds. This is an area that needs more study.

Commercial Mixtures

There are now commercial instant nectar mixtures available for use in hummingbird feeders. Some of these are powders to which you just add water. Others are already mixed as a liquid — containing pure water, nutrients, vitamins, and minerals — to which you just add the sugar.

Two black-chinned hummingbirds perched at flowers.

FEEDER MAINTENANCE

Cleaning Feeders

Successful feeding of hummingbirds requires a commitment to maintaining clean feeders with fresh solutions. Unlike bird seed, which, contained in shells, can last many weeks or longer if the birds don't eat it right away, hummingbird sugar solution is a liquid and is highly susceptible to mold, harmful bacteria, or fermentation. If you let this happen, you could be risking the health and possibly the lives of the hummingbirds that use your feeder. We can't emphasize enough how important it is to take feeder maintenance seriously.

Clean Feeders Every 2 to 3 Days

Wash feeders out in very hot water every 2 to 3 days. You may add some vinegar to the hot water to remove mold, or, for really tough cleaning jobs, use a tiny amount of Clorox, making sure to rinse the feeder out thoroughly when you are through. If necessary, scrub hard-to-reach spots with bottle brushes and pipe cleaners.

If the weather is particularly cool, it might be acceptable to wait slightly longer than 3 days to clean feeders. In hot weather (over 60 degrees F.), during which pathogens in the feeding solution can multiply rapidly, the feeders **should be cleaned every 2 days**. After you have cleaned feeders, refill them with fresh sugar solution.

When to Put Up Feeders

Most species of hummingbirds are migrant, only coming to North America in the warmer seasons. Feeders should be up in time for their arrival. The timing will vary depending on where you live. In the South arrival may be as early as January or February; in the North it may be as late as April or May. Check the range maps and migration information in the Quick Guides in each of the species descriptions to determine the timing in your area.

Five hummingbirds enjoying a feeder made by Opus.

A Costa's hummingbird, male, visiting a flower.

When to Take Down Feeders

One of the biggest misconceptions about hummingbirds held by the general public is the belief that if you do not take hummingbird feeders down at a certain time in the fall, you will prevent the hummingbirds from migrating. This is not true.

In many areas, hummingbirds begin migrating even when there are still flowers in bloom and insects available. In fact, males generally migrate several weeks ahead of females and immatures. Species that live in the same area often migrate at different times, regardless of the fact that food obviously remains for any birds that stay behind.

The birds more likely time their migrations according to changing day length or photoperiod. Thus, they are responding not to the availability of food but to an ancient innate urge that tells them when to go. Migrating hummingbirds may actually be helped by the feeders that are left up; as they begin their southward journey, the feeders give them the extra energy needed for their long flight. This is especially true in years of drought when there may not be as many flowers in bloom.

In certain areas of the country hummingbirds are year-round residents. On the West Coast, in the Southwest, and in a few places in the Southeast, hummingbirds can be found in the winter. The Anna's hummingbird, which used to live mainly in southern California, can now be found year-round, all the way up the West Coast.

Where hummingbirds are found year-round, feeders left up all year may be life sustaining to some hummingbirds. In Ramsey Canyon, Arizona, there have been reports of magnificent hummingbirds coming to feeders every 20 minutes in a snow storm. In such severe weather conditions, the sugar water may have to be warmed to keep it from freezing and available for the birds.

SOLVING FEEDER PROBLEMS

Almost everyone who feeds hummingbirds experiences some kinds of problems sooner or later, but hopefully these are minor and don't detract from the joy of seeing the birds.

Dripping

Dripping is a common feeder problem and may be due to feeder design or environmental conditions. In feeders that are inverted bottles, when the air in the bottle expands due to rising temperatures, the fluid below is pushed out. Newer feeder designs are addressing this problem and manufacturers are offering drip-proof feeders. Saucer-type feeders have less drip problems because all the fluid in them is below the feeder holes.

Whenever possible, **hang feeders out of the wind and in the shade.** Windy conditions can cause fluid in a feeder to slosh out, and the ultraviolet rays of the sun can be destructive to the construction materials of the feeder.

Bees, Ants, and Wasps (Hymenoptera)

Many bees, ants, and wasps feed on flower nectar, and, to them, a hummingbird feeder offers a free meal. They will fly, or, in the case of ants, march right up to the feeder. In dealing with ants, the best tactic is to block their passage to the feeder by putting Vaseline or tanglefoot (a sticky substance sold in garden stores) on the pole or wire holding the feeder.

Some people wrap a strip of cloth that has been soaked in insect repellent around the stake supporting the feeder. Be extremely careful when using insect repellent, especially if you use a spray. Make sure none gets in the feeding solution. There is also a commercial feeder available that has a little moat of water around the wire from which the feeder hangs. The ants cannot cross the water.

Bees and wasps may be harder to control because they can fly to the feeder. Several feeders come with "bee guards," a little screen-like device that fits over the feeder holes and makes it hard for the insects to reach the fluid.

Another tactic is to apply Vaseline or salad or mineral oil to the feeding ports; this will make it hard for the insects to get a foothold on the portal. We have also heard of someone who rubs a little Vicks ointment on the feeding portals on the theory that the scent deters bees, who have a good sense of smell, but not hummingbirds, who have a weaker, if any, sense of smell.

You can apply the salad oil or substance of your choice with your finger or a Q-Tip. Apply a little around the portal, but not inside the portal hole. Apply each time the feeder is filled, and don't spill feeder solution on the portals or bee guards, because that will attract the insects.

A broad-billed hummingbird enjoying a thistle.

Why Are There No Hummingbirds at My Feeder?

Many people put up hummingbird feeders and wait for the birds to arrive only to have none appear. One's first inclination is to blame the feeders, but actually the situation is more complex. Here are some of the many reasons why you may not get hummingbirds at your feeders, or, if you have had them, why they may have left.

— **You live in a poor habitat.** Some areas do not have many flowers, shrubs, or trees that hummingbirds like and therefore few hummingbirds stop by.

— **You live in too good a habitat.** If there are too many hummingbird flowers in your area, the birds may never bother with feeders. Sometimes hummingbirds temporarily desert feeders for the same reason, that is, when an abundance of wildflowers are available in the vicinity.

— **Hummingbirds may be around, but they may not be interested in your feeders.** Certain individual hummingbirds may develop their own particular patterns and be influenced by their prior experiences. Years ago, when we put out our first hummingbird feeder, a hummingbird came and visited our garden and systematically ignored the feeder, no matter where we moved it or what we did to it. In subsequent years, other hummingbirds have used the feeder.

— **It's the breeding season.** Hummingbirds that have clustered around your feeders may have moved elsewhere to breed.

— **Your feeding solution may have fermented or gone sour.** Remember to keep your feeders filled with clean, fresh solution. Once hummingbirds start coming to your feeders, make sure you keep them filled. If you leave them empty for too long, the hummingbirds may seek food elsewhere and not return.

— **You may not be looking when the hummingbirds arrive.** Hummingbirds spend a lot of their time perched and much less of their time feeding. If there are not many hummers in your area, then it could be easy to miss seeing their visits unless you watch your feeders very closely.

The best advice we can give you is to think flowers first. In other words, create the kind of habitat with nectar-rich flowers, shrubs, and trees that will instinctively appeal to hummingbirds, then put up the feeders near the flowers the hummingbirds are using. Be patient; it may take a while, but eventually the hummingbirds will arrive.

A broad-billed female, left, and a black-chinned female, right, taking turns at a feeder.

ORIOLES AND OTHER VISITORS

How to Attract Orioles

Orioles have been such constant visitors to hummingbird feeders that there are now commercially produced oriole feeders. These are like large-capacity hummingbird feeders with orange- instead of red-colored parts. There is even orange-flavored instant nectar now available.

You can attract orioles by placing the feeders near the trees and vegetation that the birds frequent. Once the orioles are used to them, the feeders can be moved closer to your house so that you have a better view of the birds. Orioles will accept a more diluted sugar-water concentration than hummingbirds — a 1 to 6 ratio of sugar to water. Prepare the solution and clean feeders as you would for hummingbirds.

Orioles are exciting birds, with their flame-colored plumage, melodic whistles, and incredible nests. These attributes have given rise to some of their common names, such as firebird, hang-nest, and golden oriole. There are eight species of orioles found in the United States, and on the following pages we provide

Some oriole feeders made by (from left to right): Perky-Pet Products, Briggs Associates, Inc., Opus.

quick guides to their habits and identification.

What Do Orioles Eat?

In the wild, orioles eat nectar and many kinds of insects. One account says that orioles will spend much time probing into the blossoms of agaves, aloes, hibiscus, lilies, and other tubular flowers to sip the nectar. Sometimes they perch on the stem and puncture the base of the blossom to get at the nectar.

Besides nectar, orioles eat blackberries, mulberries, elderberries, serviceberries, many other kinds of fruits, and a large variety of caterpillars and insects, including many that are injurious to crops. At bird-feeding stations they eat orange halves, suet, peanut-butter mixtures, grapes, watermelon pulp or rind, and other fruits.

Courtship

Arriving on their northern breeding grounds when spring is well under way, orioles engage in only a brief courtship. Male orioles usually arrive ahead of females and stake out territories, which may be quite close to those of other orioles, sometimes so close that they are nesting colonially. When the females arrive, the males court them with their melodic whistled songs and bowing displays. Females of most species of orioles also sing. Listen for the pair's keeping in contact with their whistled notes as they hop about the trees, looking for food and building their nest.

The Hammock Bird

Orioles have some of the most beautiful and fascinating nests among all birds. The nests are intricately woven affairs, made of plant fibers, usually built in trees and suspended from the tips of branches. In warmer regions, orioles build their nests in Spanish moss, or palm trees. Some are longer and more pendulous than others, ranging from the Altamira oriole's nest, which can be 25 inches long to the 4-inch-long hooded oriole's nest.

Even though the nest looks like the work of a master weaver, there is no organized design in its weaving. First, foundation fibers are attached to supporting twigs to form pendant loops. More and more fibers are added, with random pokes and pulls until the nest is completed. One ornithologist found that an orchard oriole had taken a 13-inch length of grass and hooked it in and out 34 times, while winding it round the nest. Often an inner lining of soft material is also added.

Orioles will frequently accept human-made nesting material laid out for them during their breeding season. Cut pieces of string or twine, of neutral color, in 4- to 8-inch lengths, and drape them in shrubs or tree branches, or other places where the birds can see them.

Other Visitors

More than 58 species of birds have been reported seen at hummingbird feeders. These include swifts, woodpeckers, jays, chickadees, titmice, nuthatches, wrens, mockingbirds, thrashers, robins, warblers, grackles, tanagers, cardinals, grosbeaks, buntings, finches, sparrows, and others.

All sorts of other creatures have been reported coming to hummingbird feeders as well, ranging from bats to lizards, ringtails, raccoons, foxes, chipmunks, squirrels, and opossums.

Depending on your point of view, you can welcome the other wildlife or discourage it. To protect your feeders from night-active mammals, you can take feeders in at night or hang them in places inaccessible to mammals. If other species of birds compete too much with hummingbirds for the feeders, add more feeders, or use wide-mouthed jars filled with sugar solution to lure the larger birds away from the hummer feeders.

A northern oriole, subspecies "Bullock's oriole," in a cottonwood.

Quick Guide
Northern Oriole (formerly Baltimore and Bullock's Orioles) *Icterus galbula*

Breeding Period: April to June

Nest: 3.5–8 inches long, placed 6–60 ft. above ground at branch tips. Made of plant fibers, hair, grape bark, grass, Spanish moss

Eggs: 4–6, bluish white or grayish with brown markings. 1 brood

Incubation: 12–14 days, by female

Nestling phase: 12–14 days

Range: All U.S. and southern Canada

Identification: 8.75 inches long. Male orange below, black head. Bullock's male has white wing patch, orange on cheek. Female paler, no black on head. Female Bullock's has whitish belly

Quick Guide
Orchard Oriole

Icterus spurius

Breeding Period: April to July

Nest: 2.5–3.5 inches long, placed 6–60 ft. above ground in orchard trees, mesquite, buttonbush. Made of long grasses, suspended from forked end of branch

Eggs: 3–5, bluish white with brown markings. 1 brood

Incubation: 12 days, by female (and possibly male)

Nestling phase: 11–14 days. Has nested in loose colonies. Also nests singly, often close to eastern kingbird

Range: Central and eastern U.S. and Canada

Identification: 7.25 inches long. Male has deep red-brown breast and rump. Female is yellowish green with white wing bars

Quick Guide
Hooded Oriole
Icterus cucullatus

Breeding Period: April to August

Nest: 3-inch-long woven cup placed 5–30 ft. above ground in deciduous trees, Spanish moss. In palm trees, sewn to underside of palm leaf. Made of grass, palm fibers, Spanish moss

Eggs: 3–5, pale with splotches. 2–3 broods

Incubation: 12–14 days, by female

Nestling phase: 14 days

Range: California, Nevada, Arizona, New Mexico, Texas

Identification: 8 inches long. Male has orange crown, black on throat. Females are yellowish, with no black throat. Birds vary in color intensity across their range. Texas birds are brightest, California birds most pale

Quick Guide
Scott's Oriole
Icterus parisorum

Breeding Period: May to June

Nest: 5 inches long, placed 4–18 ft. up in yuccas, pines, vines on cacti, sycamores, etc. Made of fibers of yucca, grasses. Sewn to edges of down-hanging yucca leaves

Eggs: 2–4, pale blue with blotches of black, brown, or gray. 2 broods

Incubation: 12–14 days by female

Nestling phase: 14 days

Range: California, Nevada, Arizona, New Mexico, Texas

Identification: 9 inches long. Male is lemon yellow with black hood. Female is yellowish olive, with some black on throat and with wing bars

Quick Guide
Altamira Oriole
Icterus gularis

Breeding Period: April to July

Nest: 25 inches long, placed 30–80 ft. above ground in exposed position suspended from branch tips in dead tree. Made of air plant rootlets, palmetto leaf fibers

Eggs: 3–4, bluish white with brown or purple markings. 2 broods

Incubation: Unknown

Nestling phase: Unknown

Range: Rare resident, south Texas

Identification: 10 inches long. Larger than hooded oriole, and bill is thicker at base. Upper wing bar orange or yellow, forming a shoulder patch. Sexes alike

Quick Guide
Audubon's Oriole
Icterus graduacauda

Breeding Period: April to July

Nest: 3–4 inches long, placed 6–14 ft. above ground in mesquite trees, thickets. Attached to ends of upright branches. Made of dried grasses, green, wiry grass

Eggs: 3–5, pale bluish or grayish with brown markings. 2 broods

Incubation: Unknown

Nestling phase: Unknown

Range: Uncommon resident in south Texas

Identification: 9.5 inches long. Male has black hood, greenish yellow back. Female similar but slightly paler

Quick Guide
Streak-Backed Oriole

Icterus pustulatus

Range: Mexican species. Rare fall and winter visitor to southeastern Arizona, southern California. Has not yet nested in United States

Identification: 8.25 inches long. One of the most brilliantly colored orioles seen in the United States. Male has streaked upper back, deep orange head, black throat. Female has black throat but is yellowish, with gray or olive streaked back

Quick Guide
Spot-Breasted Oriole

Icterus pectoralis

Breeding Period: April to July

Nest: Woven pouch 6 or more inches long, attached near end of branch in tree. Made of plant fibers

Eggs: 3–5, pale blue marked with dark colors. 2 broods

Incubation: Unknown

Nestling phase: Unknown

Range: Introduced Mexican species now resident in southern Florida

Identification: 9.25 inches long. Adults have orange shoulder patch, black throats with dark spots on upper breast. Female similar to but slightly paler than male. Travels and roosts in flocks in winter

CREATING A HUMMINGBIRD HABITAT

The key word in creating habitats for hummingbirds, or for any kind of wildlife, is variety. Here are some kinds of variety that you should have in your hummingbird habitat.

Sun and Shade

Create areas of sun, partial sun, and shade. If your area is sunny, then plant some trees and shrubs; if it is all in the shade, then open up the forest canopy to let large patches of sunlight in. Having areas of both sun and shade is essential to growing a variety of plants.

Many Levels

Create a variety of levels of vegetation. Have some tall trees, some medium-height trees, some shrubs, some flowers, and some low grassy areas. These different levels will give your hummingbirds choices of where to feed and where to perch to rest or roost.

Lots of Flowers

Plant lots of flowers, both those specially adapted for hummingbirds and others as well. Try to choose species that bloom at different times, so that throughout the growing season you will always have something flowering. Flowers will provide nectar for the birds and will also attract insect visitors on which the hummingbirds will feed.

Just Add Water

Have water available. Hummingbirds do all or most of their drinking at flowers when they sip nectar, but they also need places to bathe. Hummingbirds are resourceful in this regard,

A hummingbird habitat that we have created in our yard.

A broad-tailed hummingbird, male, on a perch in his territory.

using bits of water no matter where they find them. These can include beads of water on a leaf, at the shallow edges of a brook, or even the spray from a sprinkler.

You can also put out a birdbath for the hummers. Be sure the birdbath has areas of very shallow water where the birds can stand in water if they choose. We always put a few flat rocks in our birdbath to create different depths.

Nesting Needs

Hummingbirds also need nesting sites and nesting materials. Although it is quite easy to attract hummingbirds to your yard to feed, it is a little harder to know exactly what will make them want to nest there. Certainly the varied habitat mentioned above is a good start, for it provides the female with choices of where to place her nest.

Most hummingbird nests contain downy plant fibers held together with spider silk and coated on the outside with lichens. Your hav-

ing a wide variety of plants gives the female a choice of nesting material.

When shrub species of willows go to seed in early spring, their seeds are connected to fine filaments to help them disperse upon the wind. These downy fibers often are collected by hummingbirds to make the bulk of their nests. Including willows in your hummingbird habitat thus has two advantages. One is that they provide nest material, and the other is that the birds can feed on the nectar at the willow flowers and on the myriad insects that the willow flowers attract.

A Perch with a View

Hummingbirds are often very territorial over nectar sources. A good habitat always has some perches from which the territorial bird can survey its territory. You might consider creating some good perches with views over the flowers. In our garden, the hummingbirds most often perch on a small dead limb above and behind the flowers or on some other bare tree limb.

HUMMINGBIRD FLOWERS

Hummingbirds are opportunists and will try to feed at any flower with nectar, no matter what its color, shape, size, or position. If this is true, then why does everybody make such a fuss about red tubular flowers? And why do they call them "hummingbird flowers"?

To answer these questions we first need to consider some of the basics of flowers.

Why Do Flowers Produce Nectar?

Flowers produce nectar to attract insects, birds, or mammals. As these visitors feed on the sweet nectar, they inadvertently get pollen on their bodies. Pollen is the male sex cell of the flower. When the visitor then leaves and sips nectar from a new flower, it inadvertently transfers the pollen to the female parts of this new flower. This results in cross-pollination; the pollen from one flower has fertilized another.

The female part of the second flower then develops a seed which contains some genes from both plants. In the long run, seeds resulting from cross-pollination are more vigorous and grow into better-adapted plants than those resulting from self-pollination.

Exclusive Club

Some flowers have become specially adapted to attracting hummingbirds and to having their pollen carried from plant to plant by the birds. At the same time they have adapted to exclude or discourage other flower visitors, so that their nectar is reserved for the hummers.

Some of the adaptations accomplish both purposes. Most such flowers are red. This is because while red is easily seen and distinguished from other colors by the birds, bees see red as just another dark, blackish color and are not particularly attracted to it.

Most of these flowers also have their nectar at the base of long, thin, tubular flowers. Bees and other pollinators do not have tongues long enough to reach the nectar, but for the hummingbird, with its long bill and long tongue, this is quite easy.

Many of these flowers point down or to the side rather than up. This orientation makes it hard for bees and other insects to land on them. In addition, many have small petals and small openings at the tip, leaving no landing platform for the insects. These adaptations are not a problem for the hummingbirds since they can easily hover to the side or beneath as they take nectar.

One final adaptation is that most of these flowers have no fragrance. This makes them less attractive to bees, which are in part guided by scent, but no less attractive to birds, which have very little sense of smell.

Nectar Thieves

When bees cannot get to nectar through the opening in a flower, they often try to poke through the base of the flower to reach it. Hummingbird flowers are also adapted to guard against this. At the base of most hummingbird flowers is a thickened covering that keeps the nectar thieves from completing a successful robbery. Or the bases of many blossoms may be grouped together in such a way that the insects cannot reach them.

Do Hummingbirds Prefer Red?

Hummingbirds feed at flowers of many different colors. They do not instinctively prefer red flowers over others, but as they get more experience feeding, they learn that red tubular flowers often contain the most nectar. This is why we have red ornamentation on our feeders and why we recommend planting lots of such hummingbird flowers to attract the birds.

Carrying Pollen

While what hummingbirds are looking for when visiting flowers is a meal, what the flowers want is to have their pollen carried to another flower. To assure this they have their pollen placed in just the right position so that, when the hummingbird drinks nectar, the pollen gets on it.

Different flowers get pollen on different parts of the hummingbird. For example, cardinal flower, penstemons, and paintbrushes get pollen on the bird's forehead; Arizona trumpet is one of the few flowers that gets pollen only on the bird's chin; columbine and current get pollen all around the base of the hummingbird's bill.

As you watch hummingbirds feed, look closely at their bills and faces for traces of yellow pollen. It may help you to determine which flowers they have been visiting.

West versus East / South versus North

It is interesting to note that as you move north from the equator the number of native hummingbird species diminishes. At the equator there are up to 163 species; in Central America there are about 55; in the western states 7; and in Alaska only 1. To some extent the same is true of the numbers of species of native hummingbird flowers. There are fewer as you move north.

It is also true that there are far more hummingbird flowers in the West than in eastern North America. This is probably because there are up to 15 species of hummingbirds in the West and only 1 in the East.

The accompanying lists of western and eastern hummingbird wildflowers reflect these differences. Only those that are fairly clearly adapted to hummingbirds were included. Still, there are so many western species that we could list only about half of them.

A broad-tailed hummingbird, male, having a meal at desert trumpet flowers.

Working with Wildflowers

Creating a hummingbird habitat does not necessarily mean clearing off a patch of soil and putting in plants. Before doing this, check for hummingbird wildflowers that may already be growing in the area. If you find some, help them flourish where they are by cutting back the competition, creating more light for them, or giving them more water. In this way you may be able to turn a few wildflowers into a thriving patch of bloom.

There are many benefits to this approach, besides the fact that you save money on plants. You can learn what lives naturally in your area, help plants to grow where they have already "chosen" to grow, help our native wildflower population, and gain the feeling that you are working with nature.

Some Hummingbird Wildflowers of the West

Bleeding Heart Family
Bleeding Hearts — *Dicentra formosa*

Bluebell Family
Cardinal Flower — *Lobelia cardinalis*

Buttercup Family
Barrel Columbine — *Aquilegia triternata*
Canadian Columbine — *A. canadense*
Canon Delphinium — *Delphinium nudicaule*
Comet Columbine — *A. elegantula*
Crimson Columbine — *A. formosa*
Scarlet Delphinium — *D. cardinale*

Evening Primrose Family
Any one of many red fireweeds including:
Parched Fireweed — *Epilobium paniculatum*
Red Fireweed — *E. angustifolium*
Sticky Fireweed — *E. glandulosum*
Watson's Fireweed — *E. watsonii*
Arizona Trumpet — *Zauschneria latifolia*

Four O'Clock Family
Devil's Bouquet — *Nyctaginia capitata*

Gentian Family
Lady Bird's Centaury — *Centaurium texense*
Mountain Centaury — *C. beyrichii*

Lily Family
Any one of many lilies including:
Coast Lily — *Lilium maritimum*
Columbia Lily — *L. columbianum*
Western Tiger Lily — *L. occidentale*

Mallow Family
Texas Mallow — *Malvaviscus arboreus*

Mint Family
Coyote Mint — *Monardella odoratissima*
Mintleaf Beebalm — *Monarda menthifolia*
Scarlet Betony — *Stachys coccinea*
Scarlet Sage — *Salvia* spp.

Morning Glory Family
Scarlet Creeper — *Ipomoea hederifolia*

Pea Family
Coral Bean — *Erythrina herbacea*

Phlox Family
Any one of many red phloxes including:
Longleaf Phlox — *Plox longifolia*
Lovely Phlox — *P. amabilis*

Phlox Family (continued)
Stansbury's Phlox — *P. stansburyi*
Woodhouse's Phlox — *P. woodhousei*
Coral Gilia — *Gilia subnuda*
Rock Gilia — *G. scopulorum*
Grand Collomia — *Collomia grandiflora*
Tiny Trumpet — *C. linearis*
Desert Trumpet — *Ipomopsis aggregata*
Texas Plume — *I. rubra*

Pink Family
California Indian Pink — *Silene californica*
Mexican Pink — *S. laciniata*

Snapdragon Family

Any one of many monkey flowers including:
Bigelow Monkey Flower — *Mimulus bigelovii*
Lewis's Monkey Flower — *M. lewisii*
Pygmy Monkey Flower — *M. rubellus*
Scarlet Monkey Flower — *M. cardinalis*

Any one of many red paintbrushes including:
Applegate's Paintbrush — *Castilleja applegatei*
Bristly Paintbrush — *C. hispida*
California Threadtorch — *C. stenantha*
Desert Paintbrush — *C. chromosa*
Giant Red Paintbrush — *C. miniata*
Southwest Paintbrush — *C. integra*
Texas Paintbrush — *C. indivisa*
Woolly Paintbrush — *C. lanata*
Wyoming Paintbrush — *C. linariaefolia*

Any one of many red penstemons including:
Arizona Penstemon — *Penstemon pseudospectabilis*
Bacchus' Penstemon — *P. baccharifolius*
Eaton's Firecracker — *P. eatonii*
Mountain Pride — *P. newberryi*
Richardson Penstemon — *P. richardsonii*
Southwest Penstemon — *P. barbatus*

California Figwort — *Scrophularia californica*
Red Figwort — *S. coccinea*

Bird's Beak Lousewort — *Pedicularis ornithorhyncha*
Indian Warrior — *P. densiflora*
Snapdragon Vine — *Maurandya antirrhiniflora*

Vervain Family
Calico Bush — *Lantana horrida*
Desert Lantana — *L. macropoda*

Wintergreen Family
Snow Plant — *Sarcodes sanguinea*

A female ruby-throated hummingbird looking into the gorgeous flowers of a trumpet creeper vine.

Some Hummingbird Wildflowers of the East

Bignonia Family
Cross Vine *Bignonia capreolata*
Trumpet Vine *Campsis radicans*

Bluebell Family
Cardinal Flower *Lobelia cardinalis*

Buttercup Family
Wild Columbine *Aquilegia canadense*

Evening Primrose Family
Fireweed *Epilubium angustifolium*

Honeysuckle Family
Trumpet Honeysuckle *Lonicera sempirvirens*

Iris Family
Red Iris *Iris fulva*

Lily Family
Canada Lily *Lilium canadense*
Wood Lily *L. philadelphicum*

Logania Family
Indian Pink *Spigelia marilandica*

Mint Family
Bee Balm *Monarda didyma*
Purple Bergamot *M. media*

Morning Glory Family
Red Morning Glory *Ipomoea coccinea*

Phlox Family
Texas Plume *Ipomopsis rubra*
Smooth Phlox *Phlox laberrima*
Wild Sweet William *P. maculata*

Pink Family
Fire Pink *Silene virginica*
Scarlet Lychnis *Lychnis chalcedonica*

Snapdragon Family
Indian Paintbrush *Castilleja coccinea*
Red Turtlehead *Chelone obliqua*

Touch-Me-Not Family
Pale Jewelweed *Impatiens pallida*
Spotted Jewelweed *I. capensis*

HUMMINGBIRD GARDENING

Planting flowers is one of the most important aspects of creating a hummingbird habitat. The majority of these flowers should be "hummingbird flowers" — ones to which hummingbirds are particularly attracted. These flowers can be one of two types: those that are wildflowers and grow mostly in the wild, and those that are cultivated and can be bought from nurseries, garden centers, and seed catalogs. In this section we will cover cultivated hummingbird plants.

A patch of cardinal flower, a hummingbird favorite.

How to Start a Hummingbird Garden

First, as with any garden, you need a place with sun, water, and good soil. They are the start of all successful gardens. Given these basic elements just about any plant will do well.

Your hummingbird garden can be as simple as a flower box or several containers on a deck, or as elaborate as a large perennial border. We have both kinds of gardens and find that hummingbirds are attracted to each of them.

Choosing the Right Flowers

There are several things to consider when choosing hummingbird flowers from the list presented in this section.

— Are They Annual, Biennial, or Perennial? Annuals live one year and will need to be replaced each year. The advantage of them is that they are often prolific and bloom over a long period of time. Annuals are great for container gardens.

Biennials live for two years but bloom only in their second year; in their first year they usually yield just a rosette of leaves.

Perennials keep blooming for years. In colder climates they die back in winter but remain living underground. Perennials are wonderful in garden beds, for they keep growing larger and keep coming up year after year.

— How High Are the Plants? When you plan a hummingbird garden, plant height is important. The front of the container or garden should be filled with shorter plants, backed up by plants of medium height, those in turn backed up by the tallest plants. This way you get a tier of blossoms that not only

A ruby-throated hummingbird reaching into the tubes of columbine for nectar.

enables you to see all of the flowers, but also gives the hummingbirds easy access to all of the flowers. The birds need space around the blooms to allow them to hover and feed comfortably. Thus, when buying plants look for ones that grow to different heights.

— **When and How Long Will Each Plant Bloom?** The goal is to have some hummingbird flowers in bloom at all times that hummingbirds might visit. Therefore, look at the blooming times of each species that you buy. Try to get some that bloom early and some that bloom late. Also look for some that may bloom throughout the season.

Remember that hummingbirds like many types of flowers, not just red tubular ones, and that other flowers attract insects that are an essential part of a hummingbird's diet. Therefore you do not need, or even want, an "all red" garden in order to attract hummingbirds.

Planting Flowers

Since hummingbirds are very territorial around their favorite flowers, be sure to place a few in each different area of your gar-

den. This will make it harder for one bird to claim all of the flowers and will enable other hummingbirds to visit and feed.

Plant your flowers as early as possible so as to attract migrating birds and possibly convince them that your garden is a good place to stay for a while.

Planting Trees, Shrubs, and Vines

Flowering plants includes shrubs, vines, and trees as well as herbaceous flowers. These woody plants can also attract hummingbirds, and being larger and longer lived, they will form the basic framework of your garden. Group trees or shrubs together to form pleasant clusters and masses of vegetation, then place beds or containers of flowers around or in front of them.

Many vines are superb for attracting hummingbirds. They can grow up trellises or along a fence, and often bloom for long periods of time. Their flowers are spread out, usually with lots of space around them, making it easy for the hummingbird to feed from them.

Hummingbird Plants Available at Nurseries

Herbaceous plants:

Bee Balm	*Monarda* spp.
Begonia	*Begonia* spp.
Blazing Star	*Liatris* spp.
Bleeding Heart	*Dicentra* spp.
Butterfly-Weed	*Asclepias tuberosa*
Canna	*Canna generalis*
Cardinal Flower	*Lobelia cardinalis*
Carpet Bugle	*Ajuga reptans*
Century Plant	*Agave americana*
Columbine	*Aquilegia* ssp.
Coral-Bells	*Heuchera sanguinea*
Dahlia	*Dahlia merckii*
Dame's Rocket	*Hesperis matronalis*
Delphinium	*Delphineum* spp.
Fire Pink	*Silene virginica*
Flowering Tobacco	*Nicotiana alata*
Four-o'-Clock	*Mirabilis jalapa*
Foxglove	*Digitalis* spp.
Fuchsias	*Fuchsia* spp.
Gilia	*Gilia* ssp.
Geranium	*Pelargonium* spp.
Gladiolus	*Gladiolus* spp.
Hollyhocks	*Althea* spp.
Impatiens	*Impatiens* spp.
Lantana	*Lantana camara*
Lily	*Lilium* spp.
Lupine	*Lipinus* spp.
Nasturtium	*Tropaeolum majus*
Paintbrush	*Castilleja* spp.
Penstemon	*Penstemon* spp.
Petunia	*Petunia* spp.
Phlox	*Phlox* spp.
Red-Hot Poker	*Kniphofia uvaria*
Scabiosas	*Scabiosa* spp.
Scarlet Sage	*Salvia splendens*
Spider Flower	*Cleome spinosa*
Sweet William	*Dianthus barbatus*
Verbena	*Verbena* spp.
Yucca	*Yucca* spp.
Zinnia	*Zinnia* spp.

Shrubs:

Abelia	*Abelia grandiflora*
Azaleas	*Rhododendron* spp.
Bearberry	*Arctostaphylos* spp.
Beauty Bush	*Kolkwitzia amabilis*
Beloperone	*Beloperone californica*
Butterfly Bush	*Buddleia davidii*
Cape Honeysuckle	*Tecomaria capensis*
Currant	*Ribes odoratum*
Flowering Quince	*Chaenomeles japonica*
Gooseberry	*Ribes speciosum*
Hardy Fuschia	*Fuschia magellanica*
Hibiscus	*Hibiscus* ssp.
Honeysuckle	*Lonicera* spp.
Jasmine	*Jasminum* spp.
Scarlet Bush	*Hamelia erecta*
Weigela	*Weigela* spp.

Vines:

Cypress-Vine	*Quamoclit* spp.
Honeysuckle	*Lonicera heckrottii*
Morning Glory	*Ipomea* ssp.
Scarlet Runner-Bean	*Phaseolus coccineus*
Trumpet Creeper	*Campsis radicans*
Trumpet Honey-suckle	*Lonicera sempervirens*

Trees:

Chaste-Tree	*Vitex agnus-castus*
Chinaberry	*Melia azedarach*
Cockspur Coralbean	*Erythrina cristi-galli*
Eucalyptus	*Eucalyptus* spp.
Flowering Crab	*Malus* spp.
Hawthorne	*Crataegus* spp.
Horse Chestnut	*Aesculus glabra*
Locust	*Robinia* spp.
Orange Tree	*Citrus* spp.
Palo Verde	*Cercidium microphyllum*
Poinciana	*Caesalpinia* spp.
Red Buckeye	*Aesculus carnea*
Royal Poinciana	*Delonix regia*
Siberian Pea Tree	*Caragana arborescens*
Silk Oak	*Grevillea robusta*
Silk Tree	*Albizzia julibrissin*
Tree Tobacco	*Nicotiana glauca*
Tulip Poplar	*Liriodendron tulipifera*

A Costa's hummingbird visiting a begonia in a garden.

Buying Hummingbird Flowers

When buying hummingbird flowers go to your local garden center or nursery and ask for someone who is knowledgeable about their plants. Show the person the list on page 26 and ask for advice on which plants would be most successful in your area.

You will notice that for each plant on the list there is a common name and a scientific name given. The common names that plants in nurseries and garden centers are called by often vary depending on what part of the country you live in. The scientific names are more constant, but sometimes may not be on the labels of the plants.

After the scientific name of some of the plants on the list there are the letters "spp.," which stand for "species." This means that many species in that genus will be useful in attracting hummingbirds. Thus, the list's including Begonia spp. means that most begonias will be good for your hummingbird garden. When this is the case, try to choose species that are red or orange, for they will probably be more attractive to the hummingbirds than the other colors.

Hummingbird Seed Mixtures

An alternative to buying hummingbird plants is to buy the seeds of these plants. A convenient way to do this is to buy one of the commercially available seed mixtures. There are some on the market that are specifically designed to contain lots of hummingbird flowers.

When using these mixtures, you must prepare the soil carefully, just as you would if you bought plants. If tended well they can result in a lovely mixture of flower color and height.

A hummingbird flower seed mixture made by White Swan.

AMAZING FACTS

Fascinating Hummers

Whenever we talk about hummingbirds, people's eyes light up, smiles cross their faces, and they are full of curiosity. How tiny are hummingbirds? How fast can their wings beat? How can they migrate all the way across the Gulf of Mexico? How much do they weigh? In this section we have gathered together some of the most fascinating facts about hummingbirds to answer your questions and fuel your sense of amazement.

Size

— A ruby-throated hummingbird weighs 3 grams, or one tenth the weight of a first-class letter.

— The smallest hummingbird in the world, the bee hummingbird of Cuba, is only 2 1/4 inches long.

— Hummingbirds have the largest known relative heart size of all birds. Their heart represents 2.4 percent of their body weight.

— Of all birds, hummingbirds lay the smallest eggs. A hummingbird's egg is less than half an inch long — half the size of a jellybean.

Eating

— An average hummingbird consumes half its weight in sugar each day.

— If an average man had a metabolism comparable to that of a hummingbird, he would have to eat 285 pounds of hamburger every day to maintain his weight.

— Hummingbirds feed 5 to 8 times each hour, but for about 30 to 60 seconds at a time.

Speed

— A male ruby-throated hummingbird's wings can beat 78 times per second during regular flight and up to 200 times per second during a display dive.

— A hummingbird's heart beats 1,260 times per minute.

— A resting hummingbird takes 250 breaths per minute.

An ostrich egg compared with that of a hummingbird — the largest and the smallest in the bird world.

A male broad-billed hummingbird doing the kind of aerobatics that come naturally to him.

Flight

— A male Allen's hummingbird can fly 45 miles per hour during the dive display.

— Hummingbirds can fly forward, backward, and even upside down briefly, which they accomplish by spreading their tail and doing a backward somersault.

— A hummingbird's flight (or pectoral) muscles account for one quarter of its total weight (compared to 5 percent in humans).

— Hummingbirds bathe by flying through sprinklers or spray from waterfalls. They may also flutter in wet foliage or dip in a shallow puddle.

— The rufous hummingbird has the longest migration route of any hummingbird. Some fly up to 3,000 miles from their breeding range in Alaska to their wintering grounds in Mexico.

— Ruby-throated hummingbirds fly 500 miles nonstop across the Gulf of Mexico on their migration. Before starting, they increase their body weight by 50 percent, storing energy as fat to burn while crossing.

Other Wonders

— Hummingbirds are fiercely aggressive and will attack much larger birds, including jays, crows, and even hawks.

— There are actually insects called hummingbird moths, or sphinx moths — large daytime flying moths that people mistake for hummingbirds at flowers. A hummingbird moth weighs 2.3 grams — more than some hummingbirds.

— Hummingbirds do not have a sense of smell, as far as is known. They locate their food by eyesight, investigating colorful blossoms for nectar and picking small insects out of the air and off leaves.

— Hummingbirds can live up to 12 years although many live only 3 to 5 years.

MORE AMAZING FACTS

Hover Flight

Hummingbirds can hover better than any other birds because of the unusual structure of their wings. Other birds have wings with several movable joints. Hummingbird wings are different. The bones in their wings are permanently fixed and rigid, except at the shoulder joint, where the wing can move freely in all directions.

When hovering, a hummingbird's wing moves forward, and then the leading edge rotates nearly 180 degrees and moves back again. During this movement the tips of the wings trace a horizontal figure eight in the air.

Living Jewels

Iridescent hummingbird feathers are the most specialized of all bird feathers. On a humming-

Figure-eight pattern of hummingbird's wings while the bird hovers.

A male Anna's hummingbird with its tongue partly out and pollen on its bill.

bird's brilliant gorget, or throat patch, only the outer third of each feather is iridescent. This part of the feather contains layers of minute structures called platelets that are filled with tiny air bubbles. These structures partially reflect back light, causing the brilliant shining colors of reds, purples, and blues seen on hummingbirds.

The iridescent parts of the feathers of the gorget are flat, and so reflect light in just one direction. Therefore, in order for you to see the iridescence of the gorget, the sun must be striking the feathers in just the right way. If not, then they will look dusky or even black.

The back feathers of hummingbirds also have iridescence, but the iridescent parts of the feathers are concave and reflect light from any direction.

Torpor

To conserve energy at night, hummingbirds sometimes go into a state of torpor. Their heartbeat slows to about 50 beats per minute and their breathing becomes irregular

A rare albino ruby-throated hummingbird.

with some periods during which they do not breathe at all. Hummingbirds do not go into torpor every night, only when their energy reserves are so low that they have to resort to this method of energy conservation.

Torpor can last from 8 to 14 hours. The next morning, arousing from torpor can take up to one hour for the larger hummingbirds. As they wake up, their heartbeat and breathing rates increase. When their body temperature reaches 86 degrees Fahrenheit, they can fly again.

Hitchhikers

There is an incredible connection between flowers, hummingbirds, and minute species of mites. In many flowers there are mites that grow and reproduce within the blossoms, feeding on nectar and pollen. When the flower stops blooming and no longer contains nectar or pollen then the mites have to move on. One way that they do this is by catching a ride with a hummingbird.

As the bird visits the flower to sip nectar, the mites run onto the bird's bill and into its nostrils. (This does not hurt the hummingbird.) They wait there until the bird visits another flower of the same species as the one that they left, and then they get off.

Each species of mite tends to specialize in just one flower type, possibly to enhance its chances of finding other mites of its species with which to mate. Although there are many kinds of hummingbird flower mites in the tropics, only one species has been found in the United States and it lives along the coast of California on the paintbrush flower (*Castilleja* spp.).

During the winter the mites are usually carried south into Mexico by the hummingbirds. Some have been found to spend the winter in California in introduced species of aloe plants. However, the mites' main home is in paintbrush flowers, and there is little worry of their being spread to other garden flowers by the hummingbirds.

Albino Hummingbirds

Albino hummingbirds are very rare. Albinism is caused by a genetic change that prevents the formation of dark-colored pigment in feathers. There are different degrees of albinism. Birds may have partial albinism, in which just some feathers are white, or in the rarest forms may have a total absence of pigment from skin, feathers, and eyes. Albino birds don't live long because they often have poor eyesight and brittle feathers and thus reduced flying ability.

BABY HUMMINGBIRDS

From a Bird's Point of View

Imagine what it is like to be a baby hummingbird. The sequence of pictures on these two pages shows the various stages in the lives of young ruby-throated hummingbirds, starting at the upper left and ending at the upper right.

First notice how the nest is covered with lichens and just fits the contours of the female's body, so as to keep all of the warmth inside the nest as the female incubates. While males may go into torpor at night to conserve energy, incubating females generally do not.

In the second picture the young have hatched. Notice how they are all black at first and have no feathers. They cannot control their own body temperature at this stage, so the female must spend a good deal of time brooding them — sitting over them to keep them warm.

In the third picture you can see that the baby hummers have grown feathers. When the female arrives at the nest with food — either nectar or insects — the young tilt their heads back and give high-pitched begging calls. The female places her bill far into their throats and regurgitates food from her crop.

In the fourth picture, you can see that the young have grown considerably and have stretched the nest to almost twice its original size. At this stage the young spend most of their time sleeping or waiting quietly for their mother to return with food.

In the fifth picture you can see how they begin to exercise their wings and legs by standing on the edge of the nest and fluttering. In the sixth picture, there is no room left in the nest for the two growing birds; it is about time for them to leave. Notice that their bills are still short. They will continue to grow even after they leave the nest.

Cute Comments

It is hard to resist placing cute comments or sayings under pictures such as these. Here are the comments — you put them with the appropriate pictures. *I think the eggs are hatching. This is a sword-swallowing act. Is the nest tilting or is it me? Prepare for takeoff. There is only room for one of us.*

HUMMINGBIRD MYTHS

Hummingbirds suck nectar.

Hummingbirds do not suck nectar through hollow tongues. They have a long bill, and when drinking nectar they open their bill, extend their tongue, and lick up the nectar at a rate of 13 licks per second.

A hummingbird's tongue has grooves along its side. The nectar is drawn into the grooves by capillary action and is squeezed off of the tongue by the constriction of the bill and is then swallowed. The outer half of the tongue often also has fringed edges that may help the hummingbird to catch minute insects found inside flowers.

Hummingbirds teach their young how to fly.

Young hummingbirds instinctively know how to fly. Near the end of their nestling phase they do some rapid fluttering of their wings and can briefly lift off the nest. Their first flight often occurs in the absence of the mother and usually just carries them to a nearby twig.

Their biggest problem on their first flight is perching, not flying. They have trouble perching because their feet are not that strong. Perching ability improves with practice.

Hummingbirds eat only nectar.

Hummingbirds eat nectar, but they also spend a lot of time catching insects in all kinds of ways — from the air, off leaves, right off spider webs. They eat tree sap from holes drilled by sapsuckers too.

Hummingbirds mate in midair.

The only records of actual copulation in hummingbirds suggest that hummingbirds mate while perched in dense, low shrubbery. The male sometimes dives at the female, lands on her back, and then they copulate. This takes place out of his territory near the female's territory. Most of what is thought to be copulation in midair is just aggressive contact or actual fighting between two birds.

Keeping feeders up will stop hummingbirds from migrating.

Hummingbirds' urges to migrate are instinctive and not based on whether feeders are up. They often leave when there are flowers and feeders still available. Males often leave up to two weeks before females. Some species leave earlier than others, even when there is an abundance of blooms. They most likely are responding to light level changes rather than to food level changes.

Hummingbirds feed only at red tubular flowers.

Anybody who watches hummingbirds for even a brief amount of time knows that they visit all sizes, colors, and shapes of flowers. These range from small greenish flowers like those on buckthorn to blue flowers and from flowers visited primarily by bees to the flowers that are specially adapted to hummingbirds — the red tubular ones. Basically, hummingbirds get nectar wherever they can.

Hummingbirds migrate on the backs of Canada geese.

This is a very popular and widespread myth. We know of no scientifically documented evidence that this ever occurs. There are many good reasons why this is totally implausible.

— Hummingbirds and geese usually migrate at different times, and they go to different places. Geese begin their southward migrations in September, October, and November. They leave their breeding grounds, which for many geese extend into the arctic and subarctic, and go south to the United States and a little way into northwestern Mexico. On the other hand, many hummingbirds begin their southward migrations as early as June, July, and August, well ahead of the geese. Unlike the geese, most hummingbirds leave the United States altogether and go to Mexico and Central America. Many geese begin their return migration in the spring before most hummingbirds have returned to the United States.

— Hummingbirds and geese tend to have different habitats. Geese stay on ponds, lakes, and rivers, and forage in water and on grain fields and lawns. Hummingbirds live in wooded and semi-arid areas rich in flowers.

— Hummingbirds are fiercely aggressive birds that do not tolerate close associations with other birds. When other birds come close, hummers usually chase or attack them (the exceptions being the brief moment when male and female mate, and the time when the female cares for the young). It is also unlikely that a Canada goose would tolerate the presence of any other bird on its back.

We have seen and counted migrating hummers while participating in fall hawk migration counts. While standing on top of a 2,000-foot mountain we have watched hummers pass 20 to 30 feet over our heads. These birds were always alone, nowhere near any other birds.

A family of Canada geese, the slightly larger male in the lead.

PHOTOGRAPHING HUMMINGBIRDS

It is easier than you think to take quality photographs of nature's avian jewels. People who have some experience in photography will already own most of the basic equipment that is needed. Patience and the willingness to shoot lots of film are more essential than having the latest, expensive equipment.

The photographic guidelines below will help you to begin, but you will need to modify them to fit your photographic goals. Just one friendly caution — photographing hummingbirds can be addictive!

Equipment

— **Camera.** Any single-lens reflex (SLR) camera will work, but those with a 1/250 second maximum flash sync speed and a motor drive will work better. The higher flash sync speed eliminates or reduces the chance of "ghosts."

— **Lens.** You should have a 200mm lens or zoom lens with a range of about 80–200mm. A 300mm or 400mm lens with extension tubes is even more desirable since it permits a greater working distance between the photographer and the hummingbird. This is especially useful when dealing with shy hummingbirds like the magnificent and violet-crowned hummingbirds.

— **Tripod.** Be sure to have a sturdy, well-made tripod.

— **Flashes.** You will need two electronic flashes capable of being fired off the camera and supports of some kind to hold each flash. Four flashes are even better, since they provide total coverage with light.

— **Seat.** You will need a comfortable chair or camp stool to sit on.

— **Feeder.** A feeder is needed to attract the hummingbirds. It should have only one hole open so as to limit the bird's position to your field of view. You may want to attach a red flower to the feeder entrance so that just the flower and the bird show up in the picture.

— **Background.** This can be a 16-by-20-inch board or mat that is hung behind the feeder.

— **Film.** Your film should have an ISO of 64 to 100. Kodachrome 64 renders the finest detail in the feathers. Ektachrome 100 HC and 100+, as well as Fujichrome 100, are good choices for enhanced colors. Films with ISO's lower than 64 require more light than electronic flashes can adequately provide and film with an ISO higher than 100 do not produce the rich colors or fine detail that the hummingbirds deserve.

Setting Up to Photograph

Hang the feeder from a limb or from a string suspended between two trees. The feeder should be level with the camera, and the camera should be at a height that allows you to look through it easily while seated.

Set the tripod-mounted camera at such a distance from the feeder that the hummingbird will fill at least two thirds of the frame.

Secure the background behind the feeder. When using forward-facing flashes for light, try placing the background 24, 34, and 48 inches behind the feeder. Try these same distances when using a separate flash on reduced power to light the background.

A good setup for photographing hummingbirds.

Using Flashes

The use of electronic flash is essential for quality photographs of hummingbirds. The speed of the electronic flash, not the speed of the camera shutter, controls the sharpness of the image of the hummingbird and its wings. Medium-sized flash units with variable power control, such as the Vivitar or Sunpak, work fine as long as their power is reduced to produce a flash duration of around 1/5000 second in the manual mode. Flashes used on TTL (through the lens) flash metering may not give consistent results.

When using two flashes, place them on either side of the camera and aim them at a 30- to 45-degree angle toward the feeder. Another option is to set one just above or just below the camera/feeder axis and the other behind the feeder as a highlight. A highlight provides better separation between the hummingbird and the background and is essential for a quality photograph.

When using four flashes, aim three at the feeder and use the fourth as a highlight. One of the three forward-facing flashes could be used to light the background. Experiment with these and other combinations.

The distance flashes are placed from the feeder must be measured and consistent. Their distance from the feeder determines how much they light up the subject. Start with the flashes 24 inches from the feeder. To double the intensity of the light move them to 17 inches from the feeder; to halve the intensity of the light move the flashes to 34 inches away.

At each of these distances, try exposures of f/11, f/16, and f/22. One of these combinations of flash distance and exposure should be just right for your situation. It is desirable to have an f-stop of f/16 or smaller to have sufficient depth of field and for the bird's body and wings to be sharply defined. Remember that light and dark hummingbirds require different exposures.

Where to Photograph Hummingbirds

Hummingbirds can be found over most of the United States and southern Canada. But for a large concentration of many species, the best place to go is southeast Arizona. Try Madera Canyon near Green Valley, Cave Creek Canyon near Portal, and Ramsey Canyon near Sierra Vista. Mid-May through the end of June is the best time.

This section is written by **Sid Rucker,** a nature photographer from Dallas, Texas, who has conducted many workshops on photographing hummingbirds.

IDENTIFYING HUMMINGBIRDS

When you are first starting out, identifying hummingbirds can be tricky. The birds are small, look similar, and move quickly.

On the positive side, they are readily attracted to feeders, their bodies remain still as the birds hover, and the birds are relatively unafraid of humans. These features of their behavior make them easier to observe than many other species of birds.

In this section we offer some clues that will help you to get started at identifying the eight major species. First, find out which hummingbirds frequent your area. Second, learn to identify the males of your species. Third, learn to identify the females in your area. And finally, start to sort out the immatures. Complete identification clues also accompany photographs in the individual species accounts. Identification information for other species is found on pages 80–87.

Which Hummingbirds Are Found in My Area?

There are eight major species of hummingbirds that breed in North America. Only one of these species, the ruby-throated hummingbird, lives in the Midwest and East. All seven others live in the West.

If you live along the West Coast or in the Southwest you may see all seven hummingbirds over the course of a year. Some may breed near you and others may migrate through. If you live in the western mountains, you will see only four species.

There are eight additional species of hummingbirds that enter the United States, but these are mostly seen in small areas of Arizona, New Mexico, and Texas.

The accompanying list will help you determine which species are found in your area and thus how many hummingbirds you need to know.

In the individual species accounts, pages 44–87, the eight major species are treated first; brief descriptions of the other eight species follow.

Eastern and Midwestern Hummingbirds
Ruby-throated

Western Mountain Hummingbirds
Black-chinned
Broad-tailed
Calliope
Rufous

West Coast Hummingbirds

Allen's	Calliope
Anna's	Costa's
Black-chinned	Rufous
Broad-tailed	

Southwestern Hummingbirds

(Common)	(Uncommon)
Allen's	Berylline
Anna's	Lucifer
Black-chinned	Violet-crowned
Blue-throated	White-eared
Broad-billed	
Broad-tailed	
Calliope	
Costa's	
Magnificent	

Gulf Coast Hummingbirds
Buff-bellied
Ruby-throated

Learning to Identify the Eight Major Males

The males of the eight major species are quite distinct from one another and therefore are fairly easy to distinguish. These males all have bright iridescent feathers on their gorgets (throats), which in some cases are distinctive enough to identify the birds. In other cases you need to use additional clues. Remember that the iridescence only shows when light reflects off it in just the right way; in other lights the feathers look black.

Start by looking at the pictures of the birds in the following sections and reading the identification clues in the captions. Then use the list on the right to learn additional ways to sort them out.

Anna's and Costa's: The only ones to have iridescence on the *top of their heads* as well as on their throats. **Anna's** has *rose* iridescence; **Costa's** has *purple* iridescence.

Calliope: The only one to have *separate streaks* of purple iridescence on its throat.

Black-chinned: The only one to have a *black chin* then a band of purple iridescence on its throat.

Rufous and Allen's: The only ones with rufous sides and tails. Both make whistling sound with wings when flying. **Allen's** has an *all-green back*; **Rufous** has a *rufous back,* sometimes with flecks of green. Throats are orange-red.

Ruby-throat and Broad-tailed: Look *very similar*, with red throats and green heads and backs. **Broad-tailed** makes *high-pitched trill* with wings in flight, **Ruby-throat** *does not.* Broad-tailed is western, Ruby-throat is eastern; ranges do not overlap.

Learning to Identify the Eight Major Females

The next stage of identification is to learn how to recognize the adult females. All the females of the eight major species can be told from adult males by their clear or only slightly marked throats as opposed to the all-dark throats of the males. All of these females also have white tips to their outer tail feathers, whereas the males' tail feathers are all dark.

In many cases you will not be able to distinguish between species when looking at females. The accompanying chart will help you know which females you can identify and which you cannot.

Black-chinned, Costa's, and Ruby-throat: All have clear white breasts and green backs. *Not easily distinguished in the field.* Ranges overlap only in the Southwest and central Texas.

Allen's and Rufous: Both have rufous on the sides and tail and some flecks of red on the throat. *Cannot be told apart in the field.*

Calliope and Broad-tailed: Similar to Allen's and Rufous but with less rufous on the sides and tail. **Calliope** is 0.5–0.75 inches *smaller* than other species. *Not easily distinguished in the field.*

Anna's: Green back, no rufous coloring and *red spotting on the throat* that may form a small patch.

About Immatures

Immature birds are those that have been born within the year and that have not yet gone through their first late-summer molt into adult plumage. Immature females look just like adult females, but immature males usually have plumage halfway between that of the male and that of the female. Immature males also have white tips to their tail feathers just like adult females. To work on their identification, we recommend that you use some of the excellent field guides listed under "Resources," pages 88–89.

WATCHING HUMMINGBIRD BEHAVIOR

Once you attract hummingbirds, be sure to stop and enjoy their behavior. After all, they are wonderful little birds with lives so different from our own that once you start really observing their actions you will discover a life-long source of challenge and enrichment.

In the following accounts, we present many of the interesting and observable details of the lives of each species. But there are many behaviors common to hummingbirds that need to be mentioned, in order to give you a framework in which you can better interpret what you see. These fall under the headings of migration, territory, courtship, vocalizations, visual displays, and feeder behavior.

Timing of Breeding and Migration

One feature of hummingbird behavior that is different from that of many of our other common birds is the timing of their migrations. We expect most songbirds to fly south in fall, winter there, and then migrate north in the spring to breed in our areas in the summer.

Many hummingbirds' times of breeding and migration fit into the seasons in a different way. For example, the Allen's, Costa's, and rufous hummingbirds start their northward migration during January and February, what most of us would still call winter. The Allen's and rufous then start their southward migration in May or June, what most of us would call early summer. Thus, these hummingbirds start south when many of our songbirds are still returning north.

Also, some of our hummingbirds, such as the Anna's and in some cases possibly the Costa's, start breeding in December, a good five months before many of our songbirds.

It is important to remember how different the timing of a hummingbird's life cycle can be when you try to interpret the things you see them do.

Seasonal Movements

The movements of hummingbirds vary depending on the species, the time of year, and the stage of breeding.

Most of our hummingbirds spend their non-breeding season south of Canada and the United States. These birds have long migration flights, some going more than thousands of miles. The rufous hummingbird has the longest migration route, from Alaska all the way to northern and central Mexico.

Costa's, Anna's, and a small population of Allen's hummingbirds are year-round residents in parts of their range. During the non-breeding season some of the birds disperse from these areas and then return when the breeding season starts.

All of our hummingbirds make shorter movements just after the breeding season, mostly in response to the sequence of blooming in different habitats. As some flowers finish blooming and others start, the birds move to take advantage of these new, fresh nectar sources. In the West this often means moving to higher elevations in the mountains, where the snows melt and the earliest flowers bloom later in the season.

Migration Routes

The northward and southward migration routes of several mountain species differ. The rufous, calliope, broad-tailed, and black-chinned hummingbirds migrate north at lower altitudes or along the coast where there are then lots of flowers in bloom. The birds fly

A male calliope hummingbird with full gorget display flies in front of a female calliope hummingbird.

south at higher elevations and on an inland route that takes them along mountain ridges, where they can feed on alpine wildflower meadows that are still in the height of their blooming.

Territory Formation

With most songbirds, we are used to the breeding pattern of males arriving first, setting up territories, attracting females to them, and then disbanding the territory once breeding is finished.

This pattern does not hold true for hummingbirds. Males do generally arrive on the breeding ground first and set up territories, but when females arrive they set up their own separate territories that will include the nest site.

Males are aggressive toward almost all other birds that enter their territories, including at first females of their own species. Females defend their breeding territories to a lesser extent, partly because they need to devote much of their time to nest-building and raising young.

Male territories may shift over the course of the breeding season due to some flowers' fad-

ing and some flowers' coming into bloom.

Hummingbirds can also be strongly territorial during migration; they tend to stop over along their routes at large patches of flowers or feeders. They stay at these spots building up fat reserves before they continue on their flight. These resources are thus very important to them and they try to defend them whenever possible for the brief time that they are there.

Sorting out who has what kind of territory can be complex, since you may have several species migrating through an area and forming temporary feeding territories, while another species has already established breeding territories in the same spot. This occurs most often along the West Coast, where the Anna's, Allen's, and Costa's are breeding when rufous, black-chinned, calliope, and broad-tailed hummingbirds are migrating through.

Courtship

It is important to preface any remarks about hummingbird courtship behavior with the fact that very little is known about this behavior in many of our North American species. Much more study needs to be done.

Given what is known about a few species, especially the Anna's hummingbird, there seem to be some patterns of courtship that probably apply to all eight major North American species. After establishing a separate territory, the female comes to the male territory, probably attracted by nectar or nesting materials there. At first the male may be aggressive toward her and chase her. Then he may do one or more aerial displays in front of her, such as the dive display or shuttle display.

Following this, she may lead the male away from his territory nearer to hers, and initiate copulation. This takes place while the birds are perched. After copulation, the male returns to his territory. He mates with other females while the female starts nesting. It is not known whether she mates with more than one male, but it is certainly possible.

Thus, you will rarely see male and female spending much time together, or indeed any two hummingbirds spending much time together unless it is a female and her young, or young sibling birds after they have just become independent of their mother.

Nesting

Females do all nesting and raising of young on their own and will generally chase any other hummingbird away from the area of the nest. Nests are constructed of downy fibers and other bits of plant material, often tied together with spider or insect silk and in most cases covered on the outside with lichens.

The female usually lays just 2 eggs, incubates them for 2 to 2 1/2 weeks, then feeds the hatched babies in the nest for about 3 weeks. Little is known about what happens to the young after they leave the nest. What is known is discussed in the species accounts.

There are several features of the nest that are particularly interesting. One is that nests are often built in successive years on the same spot, right on top of the last year's foundation. This results in a layered appearance at the base of the nest. Another striking feature of the nest is that there are often black spots on the rim or around the area of the nest. These are feces from either the adult or young. When defecating, the birds back up to the edge of the nest. The adult ejects its feces away from the nest; the young drop them on the nest rim.

Sounds

Hummingbird vocal structures are not as complex as those of most of our songbirds. Because of this, their vocalizations are usually just buzzes or chatterings. Complex melodious song does not occur in any of our hummingbirds.

However, hummingbirds do make many sounds with their wings while flying. These are generally done more by males than females and occur during displays and aggressive interactions. In many cases, it is still not known whether the sounds in the courtship displays are made by the wings or the voice.

Visual Displays

Hummingbirds use many visual displays to communicate with each other. Some displays are given while perched and others while flying. Perched displays usually involve spreading out of the gorget feathers, the feathers on the neck, in such a way that their iridescence will be seen by the bird to which they are communicating.

Another display that can be done while perched is tail-spreading. This seems to be done more by females and young birds than by adult males, since it highlights the white tips of their tail feathers. Our adult males do not have white tips on their feathers, with the exception of the blue-throated hummingbird of the Southwest, where both male and female have white-tipped tail feathers.

Aerial displays are of two basic types. One is a shuttle-flight display, where the bird flies back and forth in a short horizontal arc in front of another bird. In these displays the tail and gorget may be spread for added emphasis.

The other aerial display is the dive display, done as far as is known only by the males. In this display the bird does a series of oval-shaped or U-shaped dives, often accompanied at certain key points by wing or vocal sounds. Diagrams of each species' dive display are in the following species accounts.

Very little is known about the meaning of

A female Anna's hummingbird incubating eggs in the nest.

these displays, except that in most cases they seem to be aggressive. It used to be assumed that the dive displays were courtship related, but it is now believed that they are mostly aggressive in intent and done to other males as well as females. It also used to be assumed that the shuttle display was only done by the male and more often in the line of courtship. It is now known that both sexes do this display and that it is often done in aggressive interactions.

It could be that these displays have different meanings in different contexts, being a part of territorial defense *or* courtship, depending on the circumstances.

Behavior at Feeders

Most of the behavior at feeders is aggressive — after all, the feeder is an endless supply of rich nectar all at one spot. It is a hummingbird's idea of heaven.

Any hummingbird that finds a feeder will try to monopolize it by chasing other hummingbirds away. As other hummingbirds arrive on the scene, they will either challenge the first bird for the whole feeder or just sneak in when the other bird is away and steal food.

When too many hummingbirds are assembled at one feeder, no individual will be able to defend it, and they may all feed at it with just brief chases occurring every so often.

Certain species seem to be more aggressive at feeders than others, including the Anna's and rufous hummingbirds. But there are no fixed rules as to who wins at the feeder. The best advice is to watch for yourself and keep track of the interactions.

Care at Nests

Obviously we all love hummingbirds and would like to have more and more of them around. Therefore, if you find a female nesting, it is important to take care and try not to disturb her. If your actions are making her leave the nest or not approach the young with food, then you are jeopardizing her chance of having a successful brood. In this case, move and stay back far enough so that she will go about her normal activities without concern. Watch with binoculars from a distance; you will see lots and will not disturb her.

ALLEN'S HUMMINGBIRD

Selasphorus sasin

Who Was Allen?

The Allen's hummingbird is named after Charles Andrew Allen (1841–1930), a naturalist born in Milton, Massachusetts, who later in his life moved to California, finding the climate there more favorable to his health. He made collections of many natural history objects and sent some specimens back to other naturalists in the East.

One of these was a specimen of a California hummingbird that a scientist named H. W. Henshaw thought was a brand-new species.

Allen's Hummingbird Range Map

Breeding Season, Feb. - July

All Year: Channel Islands, Palos Verdes Peninsula

Henshaw named it *Selasphorus alleni,* in honor of the the man who had collected it. Later it was found that this species had already been described and given the scientific name of *Selasphorus sasin*. As is the rule with scientific names, the first name given to a new species is usually the one that stands. Thus, the name *alleni* was dropped in favor of *sasin*, but the common name, for which there are no fixed rules, remains in honor of Charles Andrew Allen.

Chasing Hawks

During the breeding season, males defend territories in mixed shrubs and woods located in coastal canyons or at the edges of small openings in wooded areas. Males usually perch on a twig that gives them a good view over their land and from which intruders are chased out, this chase being accompanied by the hummer's chirping sounds. Allen's hummingbirds have even been seen chasing red-tailed hawks and American kestrels from their territories.

Allen's hummingbird territories are often located in small, isolated openings in wooded areas that are shielded from one another by taller vegetation. Therefore, there are fewer territorial squabbles between neighbors in this species.

At times the males make circular flights over their territories, possibly to help announce their presence to females or other males. These flights are accompanied by a louder humming wing noise than is created in normal flight. Males also occasionally show up in the area of a female's nest and display there, but they then return quickly to their own territory. Why they do this is still not known.

Allen's hummingbird, male.
Note the rufous sides and tail, orange-red throat. Its *all-green back* distinguishes it from the rufous hummingbird. Length 3.75 inches.

Spectacular Dive Display

The dive display of the Allen's hummingbird is the U-shaped type, with the bird rising about twenty-five feet on either side of the U. At the top of each side of the U the bird shakes its wings, creating a high-pitched sound. Several tracings of the U occur before the bird flies 75 to 100 feet high in a slow, spiraling manner and then dives down. At the bottom of the dive the bird gives a rough, whistling sound for a second or more.

This marvelous display may be repeated several times in a row and is done to female Allen's hummingbirds as well as other intruders. The female, when displayed at, often responds with a "zeet" call, and the male may chase after her.

Allen's hummingbirds also do the typical shuttle display, in which the bird flies back and forth in a short, horizontal arc of several feet, in front of an intruder or possible mate.

Shy Nester

You may not find Allen's hummingbirds nesting around your home, for they prefer more isolated habitats. Allen's females are also wary of human presence around their nest and will leave and start giving their "tick" call from nearby perches if you get too near. This is a good sign that you must back up or leave so as not to disturb the female as she tries to raise her family.

The nests of Allen's hummingbirds are somewhat larger than those of other hummingbirds and may straddle a branch rather than being built right on top of it. They can be placed from a few inches to 50 feet above the ground and are built in tangles of low vines or trees. For lower nest sites, wild blackberry bushes or the fronds of ferns are used.

Moss, dried weed stems, willow down, dried leaves, dog or horse hair, a few feathers, and insect or spider silk are some of the materials that make up the body of the nest. Lichens are

Allen's hummingbird, female.
Look for rufous coloring on the sides and tail, and flecks of iridescence on the throat. Cannot be distinguished from the rufous hummingbird female in the field.

often used on the outside. The remains of a nest from a previous year may form the base of a nest in the following year.

When first starting to build her nest, the female hovers over the nest site as she carefully applies spider silk and plant materials. These form a sticky base on which to build the nest rim. Later, she perches to add material. When she places the final downy material on the floor of the nest she may pack it down with rapid tamping of her feet.

In some cases, the female starts laying eggs while the nest is still just a shallow cup; in other cases the nest is more complete. She usually continues to add material to the nest right up until the young leave.

Staying Clear of the Male

The females nest in wooded areas, often using live oaks or pines. They usually pick nest sites that are well away from male territories, possibly to avoid interference by the males. Females that nest near males or good feeding sites where there are lots of hummingbirds

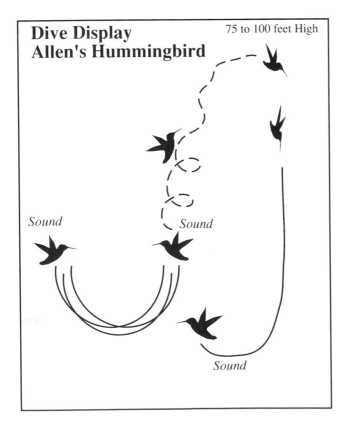

**Dive Display
Allen's Hummingbird**

75 to 100 feet High

Sound

Sound

Sound

may be displayed at or briefly chased by them.

Thus, when nesting in eucalyptus trees, whose blossoms are very attractive to hummingbirds, they chose trees with fewer blooms so that they are left alone while raising their young.

For a few days before egg-laying, the female may sit on the nest as if incubating. This behavior is called pseudo-incubation and is done by many other birds as well, including bald eagles. It is not known why they do this.

Two eggs are laid up to two days apart and, although some incubation occurs after the laying of the first egg, it becomes more consistent after the second egg is laid. The female attends the nest closely and is rarely away for longer than about 5 minutes.

A Special Subspecies

Allen's hummingbirds breed along the West Coast, from California into southern Oregon. Almost all of the population is migratory, leaving the United States for central Mexico after breeding and then returning the next year.

However, on the Channel Islands, located just off the southern coast of California, there is a population of Allen's hummingbirds that is slightly larger than the mainland birds. These birds have been designated a subspecies of *Selasphorus sasin* called *Selasphorus sasin sedentarius*. They are called *sedentarius* because they are year-round residents and do not migrate. In fact, some of these birds have taken up residence on the mainland on the Palos Verdes Peninsula.

In fall and early winter, these birds defend small territories around native fuchsia plants that are in bloom at that time. The plants are an extremely important resource since very few other flowers provide them with enough nectar until later in the season.

North by Coast, South by Mountains

The migrations of Allen's hummingbirds occur substantially earlier than those of most other hummingbirds — their northward journey starting as early as January and their southward trip in mid-May. Their route is roughly oval, with the birds moving rapidly up the West Coast and moving more leisurely south along the foothills of the Sierras. With this route they take advantage of the habitats with the greatest number of blooms in each during their period of migration.

It is believed that adult males leave the breeding grounds first, followed after two weeks by adult and juvenile females, who are followed in turn about two weeks later by the juvenile males.

Quick Guide **Allen's Hummingbird**

Breeding Period: Mid-February to early July
Male Breeding Territory: About 1/4 acre
Nest-Building
  Materials: Moss, plant down, spider silk, hair, lichens
  Placement: 1–50 feet above ground
Eggs: 2, pure white
Incubation: 15–17 days
Nestling Phase: 22–25 days
Fledgling Phase: Not known
Broods: 1– 2
Migration
  Northward: January through March
  Southward: Mid-May through September
Non-Breeding Range: Central Mexico

ANNA'S HUMMINGBIRD

Calypte anna

Who Was Anna?

In France, in the early 1800s, there lived a nobleman by the name and title of Prince François Victor Massena who was intensely interested in natural history. One of his favorite hobbies was collecting specimens of birds and, in fact, in all of Europe he had one of the largest private collections of stuffed birds, many of which were hummingbirds gathered from North and South America.

Anna's Hummingbird Range Map

Non-Breeding Season, Jul. - Nov.

All Year   **X** = Regular winter records

François's wife was the lovely Anna de Belle Massena. John James Audubon, whom the prince introduced to French society and from whom he bought a *Birds of America* portfolio, later commented in his writings on what a beautiful woman she was.

Therefore, it was fitting that Rene P. Lesson, another French naturalist living at the time, would name one of the hummingbirds in the prince's collection Anna's hummingbird, in honor of the prince's wife.

The "Type Specimen"

For every species of bird there exists one actual specimen in a museum on which the first scientific description of the bird was based and to which the scientific name is attached. This is called the "type specimen." This is an important element in the scientific description of new species, for it enables any other scientists who think they have found a new species to compare it with the original specimen.

The specimen used to describe the Anna's hummingbird came from the collection of François Victor Massena. This actual bird, or type specimen, was bought in 1846 by the Academy of Natural Sciences in Philadelphia along with the rest of the prince's collection.

One of the Earliest Breeders

The Anna's hummingbird breeds all along the West Coast and inland into southwestern Arizona. Unlike most of our other hummingbirds, the Anna's hummingbird is a year-round resident throughout most of its large range. After breeding it usually wanders only slightly in search of areas with favorable flowers on which to feed.

A male Anna's hummingbird perched at flowers.

By early December the Anna's hummingbird has returned to its breeding ground, and in some cases it has laid eggs before the first of the year. This makes it one of the earliest breeding birds in all of North America, earlier even than the great horned owl, which is traditionally thought of as the earliest breeder.

Gooseberries and Hummingbirds

One of the few wild plants in bloom during December, when the Anna's hummingbird starts breeding, is gooseberry, *Ribes malvaceum,* which starts to bloom soon after fall rains begin. A month or so later another gooseberry, *R. speciosum,* takes over as the main flowering plant in the wild.

Scientists believe that the gooseberries and Anna's hummingbird may have co-evolved. Both species have gained from their relationship: the hummingbird gets a source of food in winter that enables it to breed earlier than other birds and before migrant species of hummingbirds return; in turn, the plant gets the undivided attention of an effective pollinator.

In many cases, male Anna's territories are centered around gooseberry plants and the most dominant males claim territories around gooseberries with the most blooms. It may even be that females judge males on the basis of the quantity and/or quality of these plants in the male's territory.

Many introduced species of plants in the West have also aided the winter breeding of Anna's hummingbirds. One that is particularly important is the eucalyptus tree, *Eucalyptus* spp. Many other species of introduced garden plants also bloom early in the season and are helpful sources of food.

Male Territorial Behavior on the Breeding Ground

The breeding season starts with the male's moving to a favorable area and defending a territory that contains nectar-rich flowers and

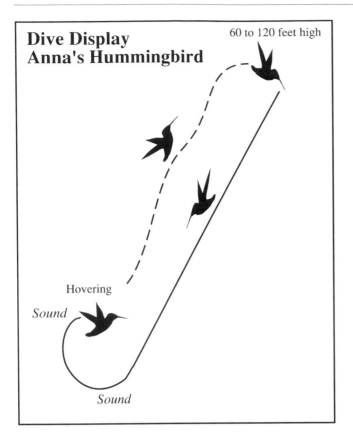

**Dive Display
Anna's Hummingbird**

60 to 120 feet high

Hovering

Sound

Sound

Getting an Angle on Displays

Anna's hummingbirds have one of the most spectacular aerial displays of any of our North American hummingbirds. As seen in the illustration at left, the dive consists of the bird's flying up 6 to 12 feet, hovering, and calling several sets of "bzz bzz bzz" phrases before he climbs higher. Once at the top of his climb he starts on a rapid descent, aiming directly down on the intruder. It takes only 2 seconds for him to make the descent, at a speed of from 35 to 65 miles per hour. At the bottom of his dive he veers up while giving a loud "speeek" sound. The dive may be repeated 5 to 10 times in rapid succession.

To make his display even more dramatic, the male orients his dive so that he is angling toward the sun. This heightens the effect of his beautiful, iridescent throat feathers as they shine toward the intruder. On cloudy days the display is done less, probably because it is less effective, and on these days it is usually done with no particular orientation.

Look for this display in any month of the year, although it is most common during the breeding season, December through June.

Look for These Also

There are several other displays of the male that you can look for when he is on his territory. In the shuttle display, the male flies back and forth in a short horizontal arc about 10 inches above another perched bird. During the display the male sometimes gives a sound like "bzz bzz bzz."

When an interloper arrives on the scene, one of the first things the territorial male does is lean forward and ruffle out the feathers of his crown and gorget. If the intruder does not get the message to leave, then the male may fully extend his crown and gorget feathers until they are expanded into a brilliant red disk facing the intruder.

In another aggressive display, called chatter-sway, the male perches vertically, his tail partly spread and his bill slightly opened. While giving a series of buzzing, chattering notes he quickly rotates from side to side, fluttering his wings all the while.

several good perches from which he can watch over his area. This territory is usually about a quarter acre in size. From the perches within it the male sings, chases out intruders, and starts his display flights. Although he defends just this area, he may chase intruders far beyond its boundaries before he returns.

Through much of the day the male perches and sings one of the most complex songs of any of our hummingbirds. One writer says it sounds like "bzz-bzz-bzz chur-ZWEE dzi! dzi! bzz-bzz-bzz." This is repeated several times in a row, followed by a pause. When another male is very close, the territorial male may continuously sing his song for several minutes with no pauses. All of the other hummingbirds in North America have much less complex songs that are more like simple buzzes or trills.

Male Anna's hummingbirds also do several other behaviors to oust intruders from their breeding territories. These include, as noted, frequent chases of intruders, the dive display done at any other hummingbird or other bird species that enters or comes near the territory, and advertising flights during which the male sings while flying in high circles over his territory.

Anna's hummingbird, male.
Look for iridescence on the top of the head and the throat.
The *rose color* of the iridescence helps distinguish
this species from the similar Costa's, which has purple iridescence.
Length 4 inches.

Baby Food

As any good parent knows, a diet of sugar and water is not enough for a growing youngster. This applies equally to baby hummingbirds. Studies of female Anna's hummingbirds during breeding have discovered that over the course of the day she changes what she feeds her young. In the morning, she starts out by collecting nectar and feeding it to her hungry nestlings. Later in the day she begins to collect more and more insects, even though nectar is still available, so that by afternoon insects are the main food she brings back to the nest.

Why does this sequence, of first nectar and then insects, occur? One possible explanation is that after the long night the young need the instant energy derived from nectar to enable them to keep warm as the female goes off to collect food. It is also true that insects are less active in the cooler morning air and thus harder to collect. This pattern of feeding the young also has the effect of giving the nestlings added protein late in the day that will help them get through the cooler nights.

After Breeding

In May and June male Anna's hummingbirds begin to undergo their molt. At the same time they lessen their defense of their territories, doing less chasing, displaying, and singing. They may also wander extensively in search of rich sources of nectar. This may bring them to gardens and other areas such as higher in the mountain where flowers are blooming. The molt of the male takes from June to as late as January, whereas for the female it starts in June and may be over by October.

During the non-breeding season, you can find males or females holding territories that contain one or two flowering plants and a good perch from which to guard them.

Range Expansion

For the last 50 years the Anna's hummingbird has been expanding its range to the north, south, and, somewhat, to the east. They have been reported in Arizona, New Mexico, and Texas, in Colorado and Nevada, and to the north in Oregon, Washington, Alaska, British Columbia, and Montana.

Some researchers believe that much of this expansion may be due to pressure within the breeding range where the population is growing. The expansion and growing population may also be affected by increased suburban plantings that provide food for the birds where it would otherwise not be available.

Quick Guide   Anna's Hummingbird

Breeding Period: December to June
Male Breeding Territory: 1/4 acre
Nest-Building
  Materials: Downy plant fibers, lichens, and spider silk
  Placement: Variety of locations, often near houses
Eggs: 2, pure white
Incubation: 14–19 days
Nestling Phase: 18–23 days
Fledgling Phase: 1–2 weeks
Broods: 1–2
Migration: Does not migrate, but shifts to local areas with more food
Non-Breeding Range: Expands range to the north and the south

Anna's hummingbird, female.
Look for her green back, lack of rufous coloring, and
red spotting on the throat that may form a small patch.

BLACK-CHINNED HUMMINGBIRD

Archilochus alexandri

Home on the Range

The black-chinned hummingbird has the most extensive breeding range of any of our western hummingbirds, breeding from Texas, where it is the most common hummingbird, all the way up into British Columbia.

Throughout this range the birds are drawn to lowland areas and often nest along streams or creek beds that support stands of willows and alders. The willows are especially important since their blossoms offer lots of nectar, attract swarms of insects, and produce, with their seeds, plant down, which the hummingbirds use in their nest construction.

Other habitats in which black-chinned hummingbirds nest include the bases of small canyons where sycamores grow and suburban areas where feeders and lots of nectar-rich flowers are available. Perhaps if you put up feeders and plant some hummingbird flowers you can have black-chinned hummingbirds nesting in your yard.

Later in the season, when some areas of their breeding range have become quite dry, the birds may move up into the foothills or the lower elevations of mountain slopes where the habitats are lusher and other flowers have come into bloom.

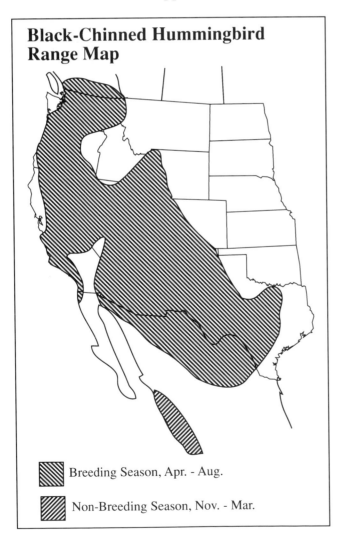

Black-Chinned Hummingbird Range Map

Breeding Season, Apr. - Aug.

Non-Breeding Season, Nov. - Mar.

Winging It

Both of the major displays of the black-chinned hummingbird are accompanied by wing noises that you can listen for and which may alert you to interesting behavior. During the shuttle display — a quick darting back and forth on the same plane, which some have likened to a figure eight on its side — there is a noticeable whirring sound of the wings that can be heard from quite far away.

Be sure to look and listen for the dive display as well. In this display the bird follows the flight path of a shallow U, flying up about 15 to 20 feet on either side. Sometimes the bird gives off a wing-flapping sound as it briefly pauses at either end of the U. At the base of the dive a high-pitched, drawn-out note is given. This wonderful display may be done several times in a row and the whole performance several times a day.

Black-chinned hummingbird, female.
Clear white breast and throat and all-green back. Not easily
distinguished from Costa's or ruby-throated hummingbird females
where ranges overlap.

Chases are common and often accompanied by a rapid ticking sound that is probably made vocally.

Territorial Squabbles

Like many of our other hummingbirds, the black-chinned male and female lead fairly separate lives. Males arrive on the breeding ground first and set up territories around prime feeding areas. Depending on the richness of the flowers these may be as small as 10 feet or up to 100 feet in diameter. They are situated in open areas that are surrounded by taller vegetation. The territory contains lookout perches and often a roosting perch to which the bird faithfully returns each night.

When territorial disputes heat up, the hummingbirds engage in displays, chases, and actual fights. In fights the two birds hover facing each other, often only an inch or two apart, and each tries to get above the other and strike down on it. This may result in both birds rising up together. Bodily contact with bills, wings, or feet can occur, and fights can last a minute or more.

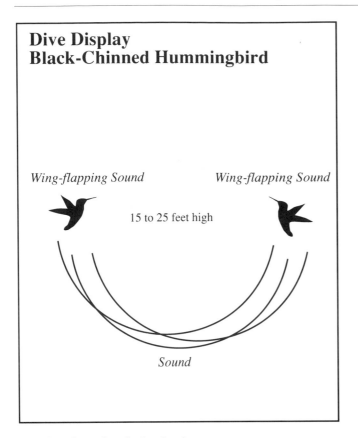

**Dive Display
Black-Chinned Hummingbird**

Wing-flapping Sound   *Wing-flapping Sound*

15 to 25 feet high

Sound

The female defends her own separate area that includes a nest site, perches, roosting site, and some places to feed. A male or female may change the location of its territory during the breeding season in order to take advantage of new flowers coming into bloom. It is believed that male and female mate on neutral ground outside their respective territories, possibly to reduce their aggression toward each other and allow them to get close.

During migration, black-chinned hummingbirds stop and feed often and vigorously defend temporary feeding territories from other hummingbirds. Access to the food is important because it enables them to build up the fat reserves they need to continue on their northward or southward journey.

Twirling Builder

One careful observer was lucky enough to get to watch a female black-chinned hummingbird build her nest. He noticed the female twirling about inside the nest as she pressed her breast up against the edge to mold it into the right shape. To mold the outside, she perched on the edge, leaned over, and smoothed it with her bill. In one case, the female took four days to build the nest.

Unlike most of our other hummingbirds, the black-chinned female does not tend to coat the outside of the nest with lichens. This results in a beige-colored nest due to the main material of plant down showing through. The plant down is gathered from willows or from the undersides of sycamore leaves. Other nesting materials include small feathers and tree flowers. The nest is a wonderful structure, being strong, warm, and also flexible. This is important, for as the young grow and become more active the nest actually stretches to accommodate them.

Like several other species of North American hummingbirds, the black-chinned hummingbird can build successive nests right on top of one another. The nest is placed in shrubs or trees and usually overhangs an open space, such as a stream, path, or road. The nests can be from 5 to 10 feet above ground.

More Eggs and More Broods

All of our other North American hummingbirds lay just 2 eggs per clutch, but the black-chinned hummingbird occasionally lays only 1 or up to 3. The female incubates the eggs for about 13 to 16 days and the babies remain in the nest for about 21 days.

After the fledglings have left the protection and warmth of the nest, they remain perched nearby for several days and are fed by their mother. For a few days after this they follow her about, probably learning appropriate sources of nectar and insects to feed on.

Fledgling black-chinned hummingbirds can give squeaky food calls as they beg for food from their mother. These calls may be heard for up to 3 weeks.

Black-chinned hummingbirds may have more than 1 brood. Sometimes the female starts building the nest for the second brood while still feeding nestlings or fledglings from her first brood.

Black-chinned hummingbird, male.
The only North American hummingbird to have a black chin
bordered by a band of purple iridescence. Length 3.75 inches.

Quick Guide Black-Chinned Hummingbird

Breeding Period: April through August
Male Breeding Territory: 1/4 acre or less
Nest-Building
  Materials: Downy fibers, spider silk
  Placement: Drooping branches of trees or shrubs
Eggs: 1–3, pure white
Incubation: 13–16 days
Nestling Phase: About 21 days
Fledgling Phase: At least 2 days but up to 2 weeks or more
Broods: 1–2
Migration
  Northward: Mid-March to mid-May
  Southward: Mid-August into November
Non-Breeding Range: Western portions of central Mexico. Also recorded in
  southern and coastal Texas

BROAD-TAILED HUMMINGBIRD

Selasphorus platycerus

The Mountain Hummingbird

If you are camping, hiking, or just traveling in any of the large mountain ranges of the West, such as the Rockies or the Sierras, then be on the lookout for the broad-tailed hummingbird. It breeds in the mountains from Arizona and New Mexico all the way up to Idaho and Montana at elevations of from 4,000 feet to as high as 12,700 feet. In these locations broad-tailed hummingbirds often nest along mountain streams, dry creek beds, or springs, and they can also can be seen feeding on the flowers of alpine meadows.

In the morning the birds may also be seen bathing in or drinking from the water near where they nest, such as the clear, crisp pools or shallows of mountain streams. They may bathe by settling down to stand in very shallow water and then fluttering their wings, or they may dip their feet and bellies into the water while hovering above it.

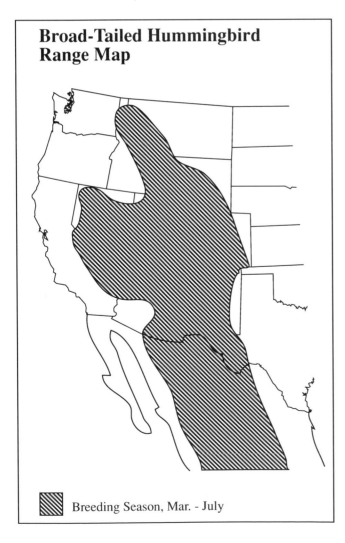

Broad-Tailed Hummingbird Range Map

Breeding Season, Mar. - July

Wing Whistle

Many hummingbirds create sounds with their wings while flying, but those of the broad-tailed hummingbird are among the loudest and most constant. The sound is created by the movement of air through the ninth and tenth primary feathers of the wings. It occurs only in the male and is a high-pitched, continuous buzzing much like the sound made by some of our smaller species of crickets. The sound can be heard from 75 to 100 yards away, and in many cases you hear the male before you see him, or, if he is in dense cover, you only hear him and do not see him at all.

One study has been done on the function of the wing whistle of broad-tailed hummingbirds. In a safe way, the researchers were able to silence the wing whistle, and they then watched the subsequent behavior. The silenced males' territory sizes decreased, they were less aggressive, did less chasing, and did more chatter vocalization during flights.

This suggested to the researchers that the wing whistle was an important part of aggressive behavior in males and that without it they were not as effective in defending territories against other broad-tailed hummingbirds and even against migrant rufous hummingbirds

Broad-tailed hummingbird, male.
Only hummingbird in the West with red throat, green on back and head.
Very similar to the ruby-throated hummingbird male,
but ranges do not overlap. Length 4 inches.

that came through the area later in the season. Wing whistle seems to get louder with the more intense aggressive interactions.

Territorial Behavior

Male broad-tailed hummingbirds defend territories from early to mid summer. Territories vary in size from a third of an acre to over an acre and contain two or more good perches from which the male watches over his territory. Many times they contain small mountain willow species that are in bloom in early summer. The females are attracted to these areas by nectar, insects, and the dispersal filaments of the willow seeds that the birds use in building their nests.

Look for male broad-tailed hummingbirds to engage in several types of aggressive behavior. One of these is a chase during which a male flies after another hummingbird until it is routed out of the territory. Another involves the male sitting on a perch and giving a chattering sound. Neighboring males may call back and forth with this metallic sound for up to 15 minutes.

Territorial interactions seem to be most common in the morning. In one study only 20 percent of the males in an area actually owned territories. The others were competing with them for these spots.

The territories are defended against other hummingbirds, both male and female, of any species, and other birds such as grosbeaks, kingbirds, and even sharp-shinned hawks.

Aerial Acrobatics

The male broad-tailed hummingbird uses several aerial displays during the defense of his territory. One of these is called circuit flight, in which he flies up over the territory and circles about repeatedly. The flights may follow a chase or be stimulated by the mere presence of another male. The display may

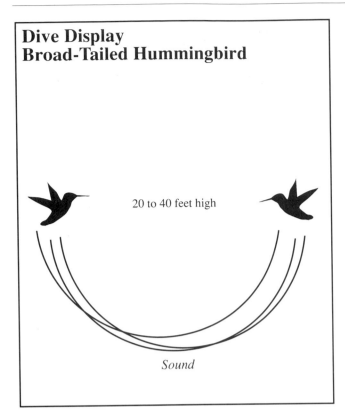

**Dive Display
Broad-Tailed Hummingbird**

20 to 40 feet high

Sound

help the male in his territory advertisement.

The dive display of the broad-tailed hummingbird is U-shaped and 20 to 40 feet in height. Listen for a clicking sound, possibly created by the tail feathers, that occurs at the bottom of the dive. This display is generally not directed at other male broad-tails, but rather at either female broad-tails or males and females of other hummingbird species.

A third aerial display is a shallow dive, usually directed only at other male broad-tailed hummingbirds.

Following the Flowers

Broad-tailed hummingbirds follow the abundance of flowers from one area to another during their breeding season. This means leaving lower elevations, where flowers first bloom but then dry out, for higher, moister elevations where new flowers are beginning to bloom.

In one case in Arizona, males defended territories in a meadow area rich with Rocky Mountain iris. Females were excluded, as were some other males that left and defended small blooming trees and shrubs. Iris blossoms are not specifically designed for pollination by hummingbirds; in fact, the birds take nectar

from openings at the bottom of the blossom, bypassing the plant's pollination mechanism. The birds also successfully chased out bumblebees and carpenter bees from their territories.

When the iris stopped blooming the broad-tailed hummingbirds moved to higher elevations where other flowers were coming into bloom. The most important of these for the broad-tailed hummingbird is southwestern penstemon. In dense stands of these plants the male broad-tailed hummingbirds set up new territories.

Nesting Behavior

Female broad-tailed hummingbirds choose nest sites where there is some protection from rain or sun, such as places where there will be branches or dense foliage over their nest site. Females will reuse nest sites in successive years when their previous nesting attempts were successful; otherwise they will try a new location.

The nests are generally placed on horizontal limbs about 5 to 15 feet above ground, though nests in places such as among roots, 2 feet above a rushing stream, and on a light fixture next to a front door have been recorded. The nests are made of downy fibers such as those surrounding willow or cottonwood seeds and then covered with lichens, bits of bark, fine rootlets from grasses, and other plant fibers. The nest takes two or more days to complete.

In one case a female broad-tailed hummingbird had two nests at once. In one nest she had fledglings that she was feeding and in the other nest she was incubating a single egg.

Courtship

Not a great deal is known about the courtship of broad-tailed hummingbirds. Mating has been seen by some observers and occurs while the female is perched. It lasts for only a few seconds, and following it the female preens extensively. The dive display mentioned earlier may be used in courtship contexts. It has been seen done by males in front of perched females.

In one instance, several males were seen doing dive displays at one time in a very

Broad-tailed hummingbird, female. Slight amounts of rufous on sides and tail; throat is speckled. Similar to calliope, Allen's, and rufous female in appearance.

small area, without there being any evidence of a female nearby. When a female got near this group of displaying males the frequency of the displays increased.

This is similar to lek behavior in some other birds, where males compete for dominance in an area to which females are attracted. The dominant male then gets to mate with the female. Such behavior, though, is unusual among our North American hummingbirds and has only once been reported for the broad-tailed hummingbird. It may be that these males have different behavior in different habitats.

Quick Guide Broad-Tailed Hummingbird

Breeding Period: March to July
Territory: 1/3 – 1 1/3 acres
Nest-Building:
  Materials: Downy plant fibers, bark bits, lichens
  Placement: Horizontal limbs 5–15 feet high
Eggs: 2, white
Incubation: 16–17 days, by female only
Nestling Phase: 21–26 days
Fledgling Phase: Not known
Broods: Usually 1, but possibly 2
Migration:
  Spring: March into May
  Fall: August into October
Non-Breeding Range: Mountains of Mexico

CALLIOPE HUMMINGBIRD

Stellula calliope

The Very Smallest

The calliope hummingbird is the smallest bird in North America. Just for comparison, a typical first-class letter weighs about an ounce, whereas a chickadee weighs about three tenths of an ounce and a calliope hummingbird less than one tenth of an ounce.

This hummingbird's small size goes along with its light weight. While a chickadee is about 5 inches in length, a calliope humming-bird is only 3 inches long. Most of our other hummingbirds are 3 1/2 and 4 inches long.

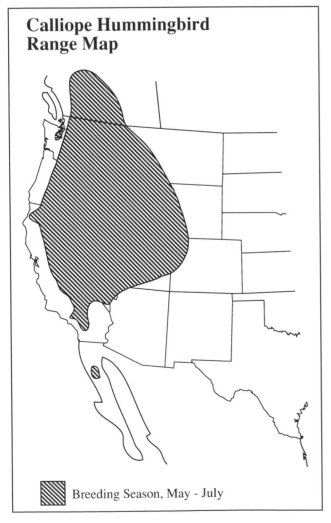

Calliope Hummingbird Range Map

Breeding Season, May - July

A Star Is Born

The scientific name for the calliope humming-bird is *Stellula calliope*. The genus name *Stellula* means "little star" and may refer to the bird's small size and bright iridescence or possibly to the lovely streaks of purple on the throat of the male, which may be compared in shape to the tail of a comet.

The species and common name, *calliope*, probably refers to the Muse of heroic poetry. This association does not really apply to the bird since it is fairly quiet and does not have a musical song, but it is applicable to our feelings when we see this bird, for in trying to describe the bird's physical beauty we are likely to wax poetic.

Reaching for the Heights

The calliope hummingbird breeds throughout most of the West except for the Southwest and the Pacific coast. It definitely prefers to breed at higher elevations and in this regard is similar to the broad-tailed hummingbird. As the summer progresses, calliope hummingbirds often move up mountain slopes to take advantage of the succession of blooming from lower to higher elevations. These birds frequently live as high as 8,000 feet and sometimes right up to the timberline at around 10,000 to 11,000 feet.

Aerial Displays

The male calliope hummingbird has a dive display that is in the shape of a deep, wide U.

Calliope humming-bird, male.
Look for the separate streaks of purple iridescence on the throat. Length 3.25 inches.

During the display it rises up 60 to 90 feet and then swoops down, making a loud whistle at the bottom of the dive; it then swoops up another 60 to 90 feet to the other side of the U. The bird may repeat this flight path three or more times in succession.

Another action of territorial males is the hover display. In this the male flies up to 30 feet over a perched intruder and then slowly descends. This may be followed by chases, dive displays, or interactions where both birds hover facing each other and spin around in a circle, giving off loud buzzing sounds as they do so. The dive and hover displays are done to other calliope hummingbirds, other species of hummingbirds, and other species of birds such as sparrows, towhees, and flycatchers.

Other sounds made by the male include a high-pitched, drawn-out note given when he approaches a female, and a soft "tsip" note.

Lovers' Secrets

There is still a great deal to be learned about what happens during calliope hummingbird courtship. It seems to be similar to that among Anna's hummingbirds. Females are attracted to areas with male territories because of prime feeding plants, desirable for either their nectar or the insects drawn to them. They may evaluate a male based on the quality of the food in these territories. By perching in the male's ter-ritory the female may stimulate displays, such as the dive display, and she may then further evaluate the male through his performance.

It is not yet known how the female changes the male's basically aggressive response to one more conducive to mating. Whether mating takes place on the male's territory or near the female's nest — as is the case with the Anna's hummingbird — is not known.

Camouflaged Nest

The calliope hummingbird is well known for camouflaging its tiny nest. In some instances nests have been found in pine trees, nestled among groups of pine cones on the branches and thus well hidden. They may be as low as 2 feet above the ground and as high as 70 feet. In many cases they have overhanging protection, such as is provided by another limb or dense greenery. Nests are frequently situated with an eastern exposure, possibly to take advantage of the early warming rays of the sun after cold mountain nights. They are also often located in woods that are adjacent to meadows where males are defending territories.

The female's nest is made of bark shreds, willow-seed filaments, ground moss, tree moss, bits of wood, lichens, pine needles, insect and spider silk, and insect cocoons.

Old nests may be reused in successive years. In these cases the bird tends to build

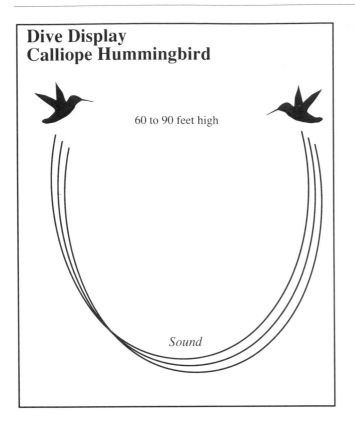

**Dive Display
Calliope Hummingbird**

60 to 90 feet high

Sound

another complete nest right on the previous one. Up to four nests have been seen piled on top of one another.

Cold-Weather Nester

Because the calliope hummingbird nests high up in the mountains, it is exposed to cold temperatures at night. In some cases the nighttime temperatures often approach freezing and a dusting of snow may occur. However, during the day the temperature quickly rises and is more hospitable to these tiny birds.

To survive the cold night temperatures, the males go into a state of torpor at night (see "More Amazing Facts," pages 30–31), but incubating females must keep their body temperature up to keep the eggs warm and the young developing. It has been noted that on the last feeding trip away from the nestlings, before the female settles down for the night, she does not feed the young, probably reserving the food energy for her own body, for she is the one that will keep the nestlings warm.

She also sinks way down into the nest for added warmth. The nest materials, construc-

tion, and placement no doubt help her as well. The nest has high walls, is lined with dense downy materials which make great insulation, and, as noted, is usually placed under some kind of overhanging protection, thus reducing radiant cooling into the night air.

The Young Birds

Two eggs are laid and there is up to a 3-day interval between layings. Even if the eggs are laid 3 days apart the young still hatch on the same day. This suggests that effective incubation does not start until the second egg is laid. The female may continue to add to the nest during the time that she is egg-laying and incubating.

For the first 11 to 12 days after hatching, the baby hummingbirds are brooded fairly regularly by the female. This is because they as yet have no feathers and cannot regulate their own temperature. For the second half of the nestling phase they can conserve heat and she no longer broods them. When the young are out of the nest but not yet independent, the female returns to the nest area to feed and occasionally preen them.

If you approach too close to the nest the female may dive down at you and make a buzzing sound as she passes within inches. In this event, you should back up so that you do not disturb her in her family duties.

Territorial Behavior

As with most of our North American species of hummingbirds, the males defend separate territories. Females may visit males to mate and then return to their own nesting and feeding areas. In one 6-acre area filled with Indian paintbrush, four males set up territories and females came in to seek out mates and feed. Another set of male territories were located among willows and alders along streams.

Male territories are in open areas with flowering plants and contain several perches from which the birds get a good view of their areas and can spot any intruders. They are aggressive not only toward other calliope hummingbirds but other birds as well, such as songbirds and even red-tailed hawks.

Calliope humming-bird, female.
A small bird with only a bit of rufous coloring on the sides and tail. Hard to distinguish in the field from female broad-tailed humming-bird.

Female territories and nesting sites are more likely to be in or at the edge of woods. If there are not enough flowers to support the females inside their territories, then they may make brief trips away from their territories to other sources of nectar.

Since all other species of hummingbirds who may frequent their breeding ground are larger, the calliope hummingbird is at a disadvantage during aggressive encounters. Other species, such as the black-chinned hummingbird, which nests in the same area, usually dominate it. However, other studies suggest that the calliope can hold its own against broad-tailed and rufous hummingbirds on feeding territories.

Oval Migration

Males leave the breeding ground 1 to 2 weeks earlier than females or immature calliope hummingbirds. They migrate southward on an inland route that takes them along mountain ranges where there are lots of flowers in bloom late in the season. In March and April, when they migrate north, their route is primarily up along the Pacific coast where more flowers are then in bloom.

Quick Guide Calliope Hummingbird

Breeding Period: Mid-May through July
Male Breeding Territory: Size not known
Nest-Building
  Materials: Plant down, bark, lichens, insect and spider silk
  Placement: Often on horizontal branch of a pine tree
Eggs: 2, white
Incubation: About 15 days
Nestling Phase: 18–23 days
Fledgling Phase: Not known
Broods: Probably only 1
Migration
  Northward: March through May
  Southward: Late July through September
Non-Breeding Range: Central Mexico

COSTA'S HUMMINGBIRD

Calypte costae

Who Was Costa?

Louis Marie Panteleon Costa was a nobleman who lived in France in the early 1800s. He was a Marquis de Beau-Regard and had a great interest in natural history, especially birds and minerals, both of which he collected throughout his life. A special part of his collection was several specimens of hummingbirds that were sent to him by naturalists in North America.

When Louis was 30 years old, a French scientist named Bourcier, who was classifying birds, named this species in honor of the nobleman naturalist. The genus name, *Calypte*, is likely derived from the Greek word for "hidden," but why it is applied to this species is unknown.

The Desert Hummingbird

Of the seven major species of hummingbirds breeding in the West, the Costa's hummingbird is the one that prefers the driest climates and environments. It is often found along the dry washes where streams have laid down large areas of stone and gravel, or in large expanses of dry chaparral.

Large Land Owners

Costa's hummingbirds form territories in areas where there is low, even vegetation interspersed with a few taller stalks of plants, such as yuccas, from which the birds can perch and watch for intruders. Flowering plants in these habitats are sparse, necessitating that the males defend large territories in order to have enough nectar to meet their needs. These territories can be very big by hummingbird standards, ranging from 2 to 4 acres.

Look for male Costa's hummingbirds early in the breeding season. They are particularly easy to see as they use chases, song, and aerial displays to defend their territories.

The males arrive on the breeding ground before the females, possibly in an effort to claim the best territories. They also leave well before the females have finished raising the young, since, as is the case with all of our North American hummingbirds, the males do not participate in nesting duties.

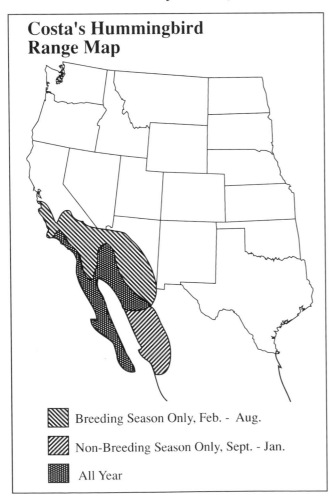

Costa's Hummingbird Range Map

- Breeding Season Only, Feb. - Aug.
- Non-Breeding Season Only, Sept. - Jan.
- All Year

Costa's humming-bird, male.
Look for iridescence on the top of the head as well as on the throat. Distinguished from Anna's hummingbird by its purple rather than rose iridescence. Length 3.5 inches.

Listen for Calls

The displays of the Costa's hummingbird are similar to those of the Anna's. To threaten another hummingbird, a perched male Costa's turns toward the intruder and spreads out his beautiful, iridescent violet-blue gorget. Listen for two sounds that may accompany the display — a short "chip" note or a longer whistling sound made up of a single whistle or several short whistles. Some have reported that younger males sing more complex versions of these whistles.

The dive display of the male traces an oval shape and may be repeated without pause several times. Listen for a drawn-out sound given near the bottom of the flight path. It is probably produced by the voice rather than the wings. Costa's hummingbirds can also do a shuttle display and when chasing other birds give a harsh, chattering call.

Nest-Building

Look for female nests near males' territories. In one case, a nest was even observed inside what seemed to be a male's territory. Despite this proximity, the male has nothing to do with nesting or raising young; he most often chases females when he sees them on his territory.

The nest is built at the edge of taller shrubs or at the edge of an opening in the vegetation. This allows the female to spot possible dangers around the nest as she is tending her babies.

In desert areas, look for nests in cacti, sage, and dead yucca stalks; in canyons they are found in a variety of shrub and tree species. The nests are placed 1 to 8 feet above the ground and are composed of dead leaves from weeds, downy materials, feathers, lichens, and fine bits of bark, all held together with silk. The female treads the material down with her feet after placing it on the branch. Outside materials are added while the bird is either perched or hovering. The nest takes about 3 days to complete.

There have been reports of as many as 6 nests within 200 feet of one another. Why the birds nested this close together and whether this is common or rare are not known.

Broods in Different Habitats

Costa's hummingbirds begin the breeding season in desert regions, where they live from mid-February to mid-April. After this, they leave these regions and reappear in chaparral habitats in late April. They may make this shift to take advantage of certain plants that come into bloom at different times in the different regions. It may be that they have a second brood in these chaparral areas, but further study of this is needed before we can know for sure.

Two eggs are laid with an interval in between of about 2 days. Incubation seems to start after the laying of the first egg, so the young often hatch about a day apart.

On the Palos Verdes Peninsula of California observers have found nests with eggs as early as the beginning of December. This is 2 to 3 months earlier than in other regions and the reason for these early nestings is still not known.

Anna's and Costa's Overlapping

During the non-breeding season, Costa's hummingbirds and Anna's hummingbirds often share the same ranges and habitats. This results in conflicts over nectar resources such as flowers and hummingbird feeders. If there are conflicts between the two species, the Anna's seems almost always to be dominant over the Costa's. This may simply be due to the Anna's

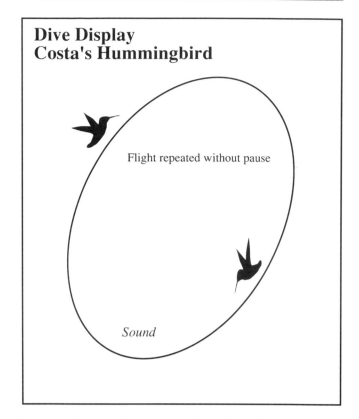

**Dive Display
Costa's Hummingbird**

Flight repeated without pause

Sound

larger size, or there may be other determining factors in their behavior that we do not yet recognize.

Like the Anna's hummingbird, the Costa's hummingbird is a year-round resident in certain areas. For the Costa's these include southern California and southwestern Arizona.

Quick Guide **Costa's Hummingbird**

Breeding Period: Mid-February through June (by some reports, or earlier)
Male Breeding Territory: 2–4 acres
Nest-Building
  Materials: Downy fibers, dry leaves, feathers, spider silk
  Placement: 1–8 feet above ground
Eggs: 2, pure white
Incubation: About 16 days
Nestling Phase: 20–23 days
Fledgling Phase: Not known
Broods: 1, possibly 2 (needs more study)
Migration
  Northward: Late January to February
  Southward: September and October
Non-Breeding Range: Baja, southeastern California, southwestern Arizona

Costa's hummingbird, female.
Green back and red spotting on the throat, which may form a small patch.
No rufous coloring.

RUBY-THROATED HUMMINGBIRD

Archilochus colubris

The One and Only

Hummingbird identification in the eastern half of North America is easy: if you see a hummingbird, it is a ruby-throat. Only this one species lives throughout the eastern half of the United States and most of southern Canada. All of the other 15 species of hummingbirds that regularly occur in North America live in the West.

Why do no other species of hummingbirds exist in the East? The answer is not known. Two possible explanations have been given. The first is that the milder climate along the West Coast favors the development of more hummingbird flowers and a longer flowering season. The second proposed explanation is that the lack of nectar-rich wildflowers in parts of the Midwest (in some areas of the Midwest there are no hummingbirds) has kept western and eastern hummingbirds separate.

Of course, do not forget to look closely to be sure of your identification just because the ruby-throated hummingbird is the only breeding hummingbird in the East, for several of the western species may wander to the East, especially in late fall.

Everybody Out

Male ruby-throated hummingbirds usually return to the breeding area ahead of females and start to establish territories around nectar-rich flowers. Their territory size varies with the density of flowering plants and the amount of nectar they provide, but an average size is

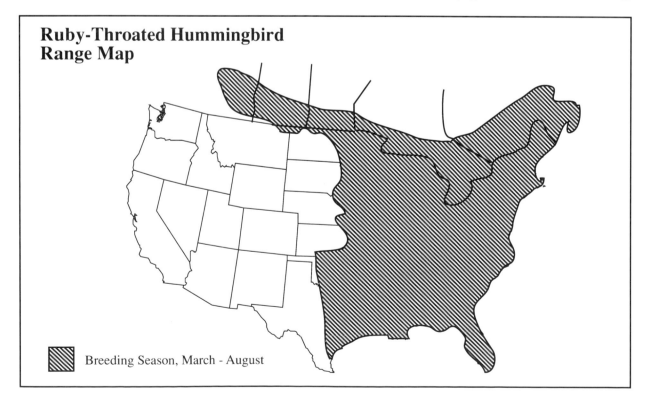

Ruby-Throated Hummingbird Range Map

Breeding Season, March - August

Ruby-throated hummingbird, female. Clear white breast and green back. Similar to female Costa's and black-chinned hummingbirds, but ranges do not overlap except in central Texas.

about 1/4 of an acre. If the flowers finish blooming, the male may shift his territory to another spot with more flowers.

The territory will contain several good perches from which the male can survey his domain. Any hummingbird that enters the territory, whether male or female, is at first chased. If the bird fails to leave, the territory holder may respond with several types of aerial displays. These include the dive display, shuttle flight, tail-spreading, and vertical flights, all of which are described in the next section.

Female ruby-throated hummingbirds also defend territories around the nest and sometimes around food sources as well. They use all of the same displays as the male except the dive display.

Following breeding and during migration, both male and female defend temporary territories around good nectar sources as they build up fat reserves for their long migration. The birds can be extremely aggressive around these resources. We have regularly seen them chase titmice, chickadees, goldfinches, and even blue jays when defending territories around the flowers in our garden, even though these other birds do not use nectar.

A Fine Display

The dive display of the ruby-throated hummingbird is shallower than that of many other species of hummingbirds. The flight path is in the shape of a U, with the bird rising about 10 to 15 feet on either side. A loud buzz of the wings occurs at the bottom of the arc.

The shuttle flight display is done by male or female during aggressive and, possibly, courtship interactions. In this the bird shuttles back and forth on a horizontal plane in front of another bird or other intruder.

A third display, called vertical flight, involves two birds' flying vertically up and down as they face each other about 1 to 2 feet apart. This can be done simultaneously or with one bird going up while the other goes down and vice versa. Sometimes you can hear a twittering call during these flights.

Be sure to look for the birds' fanning or spreading their tails. This seems to be an added message to intruders to stay away.

The Great Unknown

Very little is known about courtship in ruby-throated hummingbirds. Observers have seen males do all of the displays to females, but whether these function as courtship or aggression is difficult to tell. It is probably as is the case with other hummingbird species, that is, that male and female have only brief contact, during which mating occurs, and then the female goes off to raise her young and the male returns to his territory. Maybe through your observations you can help solve this mystery.

Gathering Down

The female builds the nest from plant down, and adds bits of lichens or bud scales to the outside. It can be built in coniferous or deciduous trees and is often placed on a small, downward-sloping branch that is already covered with lichens. The female may continue to add material to the nest throughout the period that she is incubating the eggs.

The nest height ranges from 4 to 50 feet above ground, but is usually located at a height of between 10 and 20 feet. Nests are located at the edge of a meadow, stream, or road. Occasionally a nest site may be reused, with successive nests being built on top of one another.

Too Much in the Sun

The female lays two eggs with a one-day interval in between. When it is cool, she sits tightly over her eggs to keep them warm, but when it is hot, she may simply stand by the side of the nest or perhaps try to shade the eggs from the sun.

After an incubation period of about 16 days, the young hatch. One strange feature of the ruby-throat nestling phase is the wide range of times reported for its length — from 14 to 31 days. Thirty-one days is far longer than the nestling period for any of our other hummingbirds. There is as yet no clear explanation for this range, but it may have to do with varying weather conditions and availability of food.

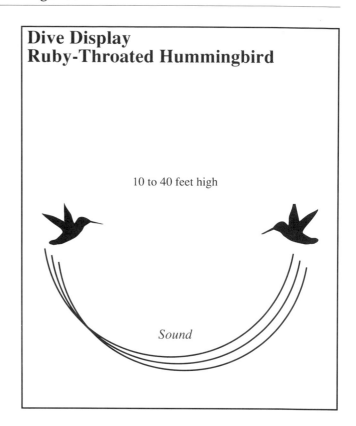

Dive Display Ruby-Throated Hummingbird

10 to 40 feet high

Sound

The young remain in the vicinity of the nest for several days after fledging and continue to be fed by the female. Soon she may lead them to flowers or feeders, where they begin to feed on their own. At this time she may become aggressive toward them, for they have reached the age when they are beginning to become competitors with her for food.

Female ruby-throated hummingbirds can raise two broods in warmer climates. There have been some records of their starting a second nest while still tending to young of the first brood.

Spanning the Gulf

Early ornithologists knew that ruby-throated hummingbirds wintered in southern Mexico and Central America, but they could not believe that this tiny bird could fly across the Gulf of Mexico. They thought that it had to take the long way around, following the coast. It is now known that many do in fact make a nonstop journey across the Gulf, and studies of the bird's energetics and fat reserves during migration prove that it is easily up to the task.

Ruby-throated hummingbirds that breed in

**A male ruby-throated hummingbird
taking nectar from bleeding heart flowers.**

the central United States and Canada do not fly over the Gulf but go directly through Texas.

The Sapsucker Connection

Studies of ruby-throated hummingbirds on migration have shown that their northward flight does not coincide with the peak blooming of many flowers that they could feed on. In fact, they arrive in northern areas often up to a month before many such plants have even begun to bloom.

The question then becomes, how do they survive? The answer is that they are very resourceful in their feeding habits and do not need to rely on just floral nectar to sustain themselves. In many cases, hummingbirds have subsisted on insects alone, and in others they have been seen feeding on the sap that drains from sapsucker holes.

Sapsuckers drill holes through the bark of certain trees in such a way that the sap flows into and collects in the holes. Then the sapsucker returns at regular intervals to drink the sap and eat any insects that might have been attracted to it.

Analysis of sap has shown it to be remark-

ably similar to flower nectar both in containing sucrose — having a concentration similar to flower nectar — and in having traces of amino acids. Thus sap is a perfect substitute for nectar in areas where there are few nectar-rich flowers and where sapsuckers live.

Further studies have revealed many remarkable relationships between sapsuckers and ruby-throated hummingbirds. First of all, in early spring, ruby-throats arrive about a month after sapsuckers in the northern parts of the hummingbirds' range. Ruby-throats have been seen actually following sapsuckers as the woodpeckers visit their sap trees. This may help the hummingbirds to learn the location of the trees.

In another case, 5 female ruby-throats were all known to use a single sapsucker tree as a food source without competing, and they all had their nests within 300 yards of the tree. In a few other cases ruby-throated hummingbirds have actually defended a sapsucker tree as part of their territory.

It is now believed that the range of hummingbirds that nest in the North, such as the rufous hummingbird in the West and the ruby-throated hummingbird in the East, is con-

Ruby-throated hummingbird, male.
A red throat and a green head and back. Very similar to the male broad-tailed hummingbird, but their ranges do not overlap. Length 3.75 inches.

trolled not by the range of suitable flowers but by the range of the sapsucker, especially the yellow-bellied sapsucker, which has the most northern range of the four species of North American sapsuckers.

Another interesting observation was of a ruby-throat following a hairy woodpecker around as the woodpecker foraged. The hairy woodpecker generally does not excavate in such a way as to create sap flow. Could it be that the hummingbird mistook this woodpecker for a sapsucker?

Jewelweed and Southward Migration

Although ruby-throated hummingbirds do not seem to follow the blooming of flowers as they migrate north, there is some evidence that they may be very dependent on certain flowers during their journey south.

One plant whose blooming time they closely follow is jewelweed, especially the species spotted touch-me-not, *Impatiens capensis*. This species blooms several weeks later than its cousin, *I. pallida*, which is pollinated primarily by bees. Ruby-throated hummingbirds rely on spotted touch-me-not as a source of nectar as they migrate south, and it could be that the later time of blooming has been an adaptation of this species to take advantage of hummingbirds as pollinators.

Ruby-throated hummingbird nest with two nestlings packed inside.

Quick Guide Ruby-Throated Hummingbird

Breeding Period: Late March into August
Male Breeding Territory: About 1/4 acre
Nest-Building
  Materials: Plant down, bud scales, lichens, spider/insect silk
  Placement: On a small horizontal limb 10 to 20 feet above ground
Eggs: 2, pure white
Incubation: About 16 days
Nestling Phase: 14–31 days
Fledgling Phase: Up to a month or more
Broods: 1–2
Migration
  Northward: Late February to mid-May
  Southward: Late July to late October
Non-Breeding Range: Southern Mexico and Central America

RUFOUS HUMMINGBIRD

Selasphorus rufus

Most Northern Hummingbird

Several of our hummingbirds breed in the North, including the ruby-throat, black-chin, calliope, and broad-tail, but the rufous hummingbird is the most northerly in range of them all. It breeds in the Northwest from northern California, Oregon, Washington, Idaho, and Montana, right up through British Columbia and well into southern Alaska. It is the only hummingbird that regularly occurs in Alaska.

Rufous Hummingbird Range Map

Alaska

Canada

Breeding Season

Problems of Identifying Rufous and Allen's Hummingbirds

Rufous and Allen's hummingbirds are both in the genus *Selasphorus* and their general appearance and behavior are extremely similar. Only the adult males can be clearly distinguished in the field; the females and immatures must be held up close, such as during banding, to be positive of their identification.

The adult males of both species can be recognized by their iridescent red to red-orange throats. To distinguish them, look at their backs. The back of the rufous hummingbird is rufous, sometimes flecked with bits of green, whereas the back of the Allen's hummingbird is all green.

Numerous Nests

The nests of rufous hummingbirds can be located quite close to one another and extremely abundant. One study found as many as 105 nests per 100 acres. This was in a forest of Douglas fir, western red cedar, western hemlock, white birch, and broadleaf maple. In this study a very interesting trend in nest location was also discovered. In spring, the rufous hummingbirds built their nests low and in the conifers, whereas in summer, they built them high and in the deciduous trees.

In early spring, the most constant temperatures occur low to the ground in the coniferous areas; in fall, they occur in the upper layers of deciduous trees. Thus, the birds minimize the effects of the environment on their nests by choosing different nest sites in different seasons.

The nest is built of moss, willow down, and spider or caterpillar silk and covered with lichens or rootlets. In subsequent years, a fe-

Rufous hummingbird, male.
Only hummingbird with rufous sides, tail, and back. Back sometimes tinged with green. Orange-red throat. Length 3.75 inches.

male may use the same nest site and build right on top of a previous nest.

By the time the nestlings are almost full grown, the nest is too small for them; it consequently becomes stretched out and somewhat flattened. You may find the rim of the nest to be covered with excrement. This happens because the young defecate by backing up to the edge of the nest and expelling their feces over the rim. Sometimes they clear the rim and sometimes they do not.

When the baby hummingbirds are ready to leave the nest, they just fly right out and perch nearby. They do not have any trouble flying but they are a little wobbly at first when trying to balance on perches. The fledglings do not go back to the nest but they do seem to frequent certain perches for several days as they continue to be fed by the female.

Territorial Behavior

Amazingly, there are no published studies of the territorial or courtship behavior of rufous hummingbirds during the breeding season. What have been studied are the temporary territories formed around rich food sources while the birds are on migration. These are vigorously defended for several days at a time before the birds continue migrating.

One observation was made around a patch of butter-and-eggs in Yellowstone National Park. Here there were 5 rufous hummingbird territories each containing about 120 square feet of flowers. The birds surveyed their territories from perches on grass stems, overhead telephone wires, or even from on top of slight rises in the ground. Rufous hummingbirds may even chase bees and dragonflies out of their territories.

In some instances, where migration routes or ranges overlap, there may be many species of hummingbirds defending territories in the same patch of flowers. In one patch of bladderpod in southern California in late spring, 15 hummingbirds, including Costa's, rufous, and Allen's, were all seen defending separate territories within an area 100 feet by 50 feet.

Tapping the Sap

Rufous hummingbirds have been observed to defend certain trees where sapsuckers have made sap-collecting holes through the bark. The hummingbird eats the sap and defends the tree against other intruding hummingbirds. One bird stayed 6 days at a given tree.

From observations, it was shown that birds defending trees stayed perched more than birds defending patches of flowers and there-

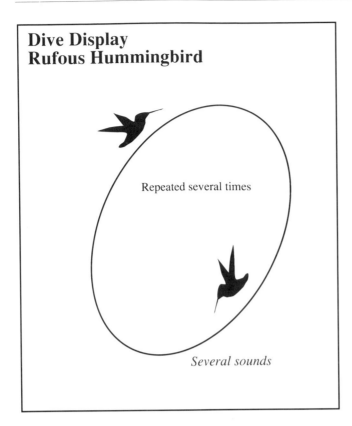

**Dive Display
Rufous Hummingbird**

Repeated several times

Several sounds

fore used less energy in getting their food. Tree sap is very similar in sugar concentration to flower nectar, and thus these trees can be important feeding places for the rufous hummingbird during migration.

The Most Aggressive

During migration, when rufous hummingbirds defend temporary feeding territories, they are the most aggressive of all species and regularly displace Anna's, broad-tailed, calliope, and black-chinned hummingbirds from flower patches. It is believed that they are able to do this due to their greater wing loading — more weight per area of wing.

A higher measure of wing loading means that you can be more agile but not as efficient a flier. This is a strange adaptation for a bird that has the longest migration route of any of our hummingbirds.

According to one scientist, the explanation for this adaptation has to do with how the rufous hummingbird feeds during migration. It takes long flights followed by short stops at nectar-rich flowers to build up fat reserves; then it takes off on another long flight.

When the bird stops during migration, it needs to be able to compete with breeding species and other migrant hummingbirds. Evolution seems to have favored the rufous hummingbird with the ability to acquire a territory easily, even during a short stop, rather than giving it increased efficiency during the flying part of its migration.

Male rufous hummingbirds have a higher wing loading than females and so can displace them from territories and feeders.

Challengers and Robbers

During migration, some rufous hummingbirds do not have territories. These birds without territories can be divided roughly into two groups — the challengers and the robbers.

Challengers are birds that are trying to take over a territory. They give chattering calls when entering the territory and fight with the territory owner for a day or more.

Robbers, on the other hand, take another tack. Rather than challenge for a territory, their strategy is just to sneak in and rob some nectar until they are spotted. They stay low and quiet and, once seen, immediately leave.

Because of their bright colors it is hard for adult males to be robbers, and so they are usually challengers. On the other hand, females and immatures, which are slightly less aggressive, are usually robbers.

A Real Fan

Rufous hummingbirds use several displays during aggressive interactions with other birds. One display is tail fanning while perched or in flight. This shows off its rufous color and, in the case of the females and immatures, the white tips of the outer tail feathers.

Other displays include gorget spreading, shuttle flight, and the dive display. The dive display of the male rufous hummingbird occurs in an oval flight path that is slightly tilted from the vertical, probably to heighten the effect of the sun's shining on the male's gorget. On the downward part of the flight, the male makes a series of sounds — a wing buzz, then 3 or 4 short whines, followed by a rattle. The whole dive display may occur several times in succession and is usually directed at a territorial intruder.

The Longest Migrant

The rufous hummingbird has the longest migration route of any North American hummingbird. Its spring route north is almost exclusively along the coast, while its post-breeding route is inland along the Rocky Mountains where the birds seem to travel long distances and then stop to feed for several days at a time at mountain meadows. Thus their overall migration pattern is an oval.

Rufous hummingbirds usually migrate south in two waves — the first is made up of the adult males, and they are followed in about a week or more by females, and soon thereafter by immatures.

Far Afield

The rufous hummingbird, a western bird, is the most common vagrant species of hummingbird east of the Mississippi. A vagrant is a bird that has wandered or been blown out of its normal range. The rufous hummingbird has been seen from Nova Scotia to the tip of Florida, where it has been spotted over 50 times.

Interestingly, most of these sightings occur in November and December, thus the vagrants are probably birds that have drifted east during their southern migration route. Some of these birds have even successfully wintered in the southern states such as Mississippi, Louisiana, and Alabama. The moral of all of this is that if you live in the East and see a hummingbird in late fall, look closely; it may be a rufous hummingbird.

Rufous hummingbird, female, left; immature, right.
Female has rufous on sides and tail and flecks of red on throat. Cannot be distinguished in the field from the female Allen's hummingbird.

Quick Guide   Rufous Hummingbird

Breeding Period: April to July
Male Breeding Territory: Size not known
Nest-Building
  Materials: Downy plant fibers, moss, lichens
  Placement: Variety of locations and heights
Eggs: 2, white
Incubation: Length of incubation not known
Nestling Phase: About 20 days
Fledgling Phase: Not known
Broods: 1, possibly 2
Migration
  Northward: February to May
  Southward: Late June to October
Non-Breeding Range: Southern Mexico

BERYLLINE HUMMINGBIRD

Amazilia beryllina

A Southwestern Hummingbird

Berylline humming-bird, male.
All-green head and throat, and brown wings and tail. Length: 4.25 inches. Female (not pictured) similar but gray rather than chestnut on belly.

Bird gently held during banding.

Rare Hummer

Of the species in this book, the berylline is the least often seen. There have been only a handful of recorded sightings. These have occurred in mountain ridges in southern Arizona — the Huachuca Mountains, Santa Rita Mountains, and Chiricahua Mountains. The first recorded sighting was in 1967.

Even fewer nests have been sighted. Many of these were located in Arizona sycamores about 15 to 25 above the ground.

More Study Needed

As is the case with each of these southwestern species, which are primarily Mexican birds who are at the northern limit of their ranges when in the United States, there is very little known about beryllines' behavior. It is always amazing to find out that there are still species of birds that have not yet been studied. This makes behavior watching exciting, for you never know when you might see something that has never before been observed.

Quick Guide
Berylline Hummingbird

U.S. Breeding Period: July to August
Migration
   Northward: June
   Southward: August
U.S. Breeding Range: Mountains of southern Arizona
Non-Breeding Range: Northwestern to central Mexican mountains

BLUE-THROATED HUMMINGBIRD

Lampornis clemenciac

A Southwestern Hummingbird

Blue-throated hummingbird, male. A large bird with a blue throat and white at the tip of the tail. Length: 5 inches. **Female (not pictured)**, a large bird with white underside, a white eye stripe, white "whisker," and extensive white patches at the tip of the tail.

Life and Times

The blue-throat has been better studied than many of our other southwestern hummingbirds. It tends to live along the edges of streams in mountains or canyons, and usually places its nest in a spot with good overhead protection. These birds have been known to raise 3 broods in one season.

Our Largest Hummingbird

The blue-throated hummingbird is the largest of all our North American hummingbirds. It is about the same length as the magnificent hummingbird but weighs 8.4 grams, substantially more than the magnificent, which weighs 7.7 grams. This added weight is probably why it has such a large tail and wings.

Another interesting feature of the blue-throated hummingbird species is that the male is larger than the female. In most of our other hummingbirds, it is the female that is larger than the male. This suggests that the roles of the sexes may be different in this species.

> ### *Quick Guide*
> ### Blue-Throated Hummingbird
>
> **U.S. Breeding Period:** April to July
> **Migration**
>   Northward: March to May
>   Southward: August to October
> **U.S. Breeding Range:** Southeastern Arizona, southwestern New Mexico, and western Texas
> **Non-Breeding Range:** Northern and central Mexico

BROAD-BILLED HUMMINGBIRD

Cynanthus latirostris

A Southwestern Hummingbird

Broad-billed hummingbird, male. A dark bird, green on the back and belly with a large, dark blue patch on the throat. Bill bright red with black tip. Length: 4 inches. **Female (not pictured)**, red bill, thin white eye stripe, and gray underside, with no flecks of green on the throat.

Where Is It Found?

You will find the broad-billed hummingbird during the summer months nesting in arid areas at the base of mountain canyons or along small streambeds. Its nests are in shrubs, vines, or trees and placed low to the ground, often out over water such as a creek or stream.

The Nest

The nest of the broad-billed female is made from grass stalks and other bits of plant material washed up along the stream. It is lined with plant down and covered with bark bits and small leaves. It is generally not covered with lichens, as is the case with the nests of so many of our other hummingbirds.

Practically nothing is known about the breeding or displays of this species. Perhaps your observations can add to what is known.

Quick Guide
Broad-Billed Hummingbird

U.S. Breeding Period: Mid-April to August

Migration
  Northward: March to April
  Southward: September to October

U.S. Breeding Range: Southeast Arizona, southwest New Mexico, western Texas

Non-Breeding Range: Northern and central Mexico

LUCIFER HUMMINGBIRD

Calothorax lucifer

A Southwestern Hummingbird

The Bill, Please

The Lucifer hummingbird is distinctive among our hummingbirds by the shape of its bill, which is disproportionately long and curves down markedly at the tip. This longer, curved bill is believed not to be for getting nectar from longer-tubed flowers but more likely is an adaptation for gathering insects from flowers, for this species eats a lot of insects.

Time Well Spent

A close study of one territorial male showed that, out of an hour, he spent 41 minutes perched, 4 minutes feeding, and 15 minutes chasing out intruders. To perch, he would head for shade and face away from the sun. Feeding bouts were brief, lasting 12 seconds each.

Agave Bird

The Lucifer hummingbird lives in open desert areas where one of its favorite plants is the agave. When in bloom, these plants supply lots of nectar and also attract hordes of insects.

Male Lucifer hummingbirds defend small territories during the breeding season, and these are often centered around two or three agave plants. The females are also attracted to agaves, not only for food but also for nesting. Many nests have been found among the dried pods on agave stalks.

What's in a Name?

Calothorax is Greek for "beautiful chest," and *lucifer* means "light bearer." Lucifer is also the name of the proud and rebellious archangel who fell from heaven. However, there is not an ounce of evil in this spectacular little bird.

Quick Guide
Lucifer Hummingbird

U.S. Breeding Period: May to August
Migration
  Northward: April and May
  Southward: September
U.S. Breeding Range: Southeastern
  Arizona and western Texas
Non-Breeding Range: Central Mexico

Lucifer humming-bird, male.
Purple throat and long down-curved bill.
Length: 3.5 inches.
Female (not pictured),
buff breast and throat and long down-curved bill.

MAGNIFICENT HUMMINGBIRD

Eugenes fulgens

A Southwestern Hummingbird

Magnificent hummingbird, male. A large bird with dark belly, green throat, and purple crown. Length: 5.25 inches. **Female (not pictured)**, green head and back, light underside, dark bill, white eye stripe, and no white "whisker."

Used to be Rivoli's

The former name of this species was Rivoli's hummingbird, in honor of François Victor Massena, the Duc de Rivoli. He was an ardent collector of birds, especially hummingbirds, and it was his lovely wife after whom the Anna's hummingbird was named.

Although it is always hard to get used to name changes, the adjective "magnificent" certainly fits this large and wonderfully iridescent hummingbird.

Facts of Life

Male and female magnificent hummingbirds seem to hold separate territories during the breeding season. Along with the blue-throated hummingbird, the other large hummingbird north of Mexico, the magnificent dominates areas rich in agave, penstemons, honeysuckle, salvias, and thistles.

The female builds a fairly large nest. It is saddled over a branch of a tree, on average, about 30 feet above the ground. The nest is composed of moss and other plant materials, lined with plant down, and covered with lichens.

Quick Guide
Magnificent Hummingbird

U.S. Breeding Period: May to July
Migration
   Northward: March
   Southward: October to November
U.S. Breeding Range: Mountains of southeastern Arizona, southwestern New Mexico, western Texas
Non-Breeding Range: Central Mexico

VIOLET-CROWNED HUMMINGBIRD

Amazilia violiceps

A Southwestern Hummingbird

Violet-crowned hummingbird, male or female.
Red bill with black tip, bright white throat and belly, and blue crown. Length: 4.5 inches.

Only in One Canyon

The violet-crowned hummingbird is found in only one small area of the United States: the adjacent corners of Arizona and New Mexico. Only a few nests of this species have been found, and most of these were located in sycamore trees and placed on branches 20 to 40 feet above the ground.

Look Closely

Practically nothing is known about migratory movements, territorial behavior, displays, courtship, nesting, or breeding behavior of this species. If you observe its behavior, make some notes. What you see could be important.

> ### *Quick Guide*
> ### Violet-Crowned Hummingbird
>
> **U.S. Breeding Period:** June to August
> **Migration**
>   Northward: June
>   Southward: September to October
> **U.S. Breeding Range:** Mountains of south-eastern Arizona and southwestern New Mexico
> **Non-Breeding Range:** Western Mexico

WHITE-EARED HUMMINGBIRD

Hylocharis leucotis

A Southwestern Hummingbird

White-eared hummingbird, female. Red bill, heavy white eye stripe, and some flecks of green on the chin and sides of the breast. Length: 3.75 inches. **Male (not pictured)**, red bill and broad white eye stripe against a black cheek patch.

Rare Summer Visitor

The white-eared hummingbird is not often seen in the United States except in a few spots in the Chiricahua and Huachuca Mountains of Arizona, the Animas Mountains of New Mexico, and the Chisos Mountains in Texas. It arrives in summer and seems to prefer mountain woodlands.

Easily Confused

It is easy to mistake the female white-eared hummingbird for the females of several other species that also have white eye stripes. The female magnificent hummingbird looks similar but is larger and has a black rather than red bill.

Female and immature male broad-billed hummingbirds are harder to distinguish from the female white-eared because, like the white-eared, they have red bills. The female broad-billed has a clear gray throat, though, while that of the white-eared is flecked with green. The immature male broad-billed has a small patch of green on the throat rather than the overall flecking of the white-eared.

> ### *Quick Guide*
> ### White-Eared Hummingbird
>
> **U.S. Breeding Period:** June to August
> **Migration**
>   Northward: April to May
>   Southward: August to September
> **U.S. Breeding Range:** Southeastern Arizona, southwestern New Mexico, and western Texas
> **Non-Breeding Range:** Northwestern to central Mexico

BUFF-BELLIED HUMMINGBIRD

Amazilia yucatanensis

A Gulf Coast Hummingbird

Buff-bellied hummingbird. The only hummingbird in U.S. with red bill and green throat. Male and female alike. Length 4.25 inches.

Southern Texas Breeder

Although other species of hummingbirds, such as the ruby-throated and black-chinned, may frequent the coast of Texas and Louisiana, the buff-bellied is the only one of these with a red bill, making it easy to identify.

It is one of our larger hummingbirds and is generally found along streams where there are dense shrubs and vines with lots of flowers in bloom that it can feed on. From past and present records it seems that the population in Texas is declining.

Males and Females Alike

In the genus *Amazilia*, which includes the violet-crowned, buff-bellied, and berylline hummingbirds, the sexes look alike (they are monomorphic). This is in striking contrast to our other species, in which male and female are dimorphic.

In general, monomorphism suggests that the sexes have similar roles. Perhaps in *Amazilia* species the male helps out in raising the young. As yet, this cannot be confirmed, since very few behavior studies have been done on this species.

Quick Guide
Buff-Bellied Hummingbird

U.S. Breeding Period: March to July
Migration:
  Northward: June to July, after breeding
  Southward: August
U.S. Breeding Range: Southern Texas
Non-Breeding Range: Gulf coast of Mexico, Texas, and Louisiana

RESOURCES

There is not space to list all the specific resources we used to create this book, such as the ornithological journals *Auk, Condor,* and *Wilson Bulletin,* as well as the many experts who were generous with their time and knowledge. The following is a list of resources available to the public to help them enjoy hummingbirds.

Books about Hummingbirds

Browning, Norma Lee, and Russell Ogg. 1978. *He Saw a Hummingbird*. Midland, MI: Northwood Institute Press.

Dennis, John V., and Pat Murphy. 1983. *Special Reprint I: Hummingbirds*. Marietta, OH: Bird Watcher's Digest.

Grant, K. A., and V. Grant. 1968. *Hummingbirds and Their Flowers*. New York: Columbia University Press.

A hummingbird visiting a feeder made by Aspects, Inc.

Greenwalt, C. H. 1960. *Hummingbirds*. New York: Doubleday & Company.

Holmgren, Virginia C. 1986. *The Way of the Hummingbird*. Santa Barbara, CA: Capra Press.

Johnsgard, P. A. 1983. *Hummingbirds of North America*. Washington, DC: Smithsonian Institution Press.

Scheithauer, W. 1973. *Hummingbirds*. New York: Thomas Y. Crowell.

Skutch, A. F. 1980. *The Life of the Hummingbird*. New York: Crown.

Tyrrell, Esther Q., and Robert A. Tyrrell. 1985. *Hummingbirds*. New York: Crown.

Videos

Hummingbirds Up Close by Michael Godfrey, Nature Science Network.

Bird Magazines

Birder's World, 720 East 8th St., Holland , MI 49423

Bird Watcher's Digest, Box 110, Marietta, OH 45750

Living Bird Quarterly, Laboratory of Ornithology at Cornell University, 159 Sapsucker Woods Rd., Ithaca, NY 14850

Wild Bird, P.O Box 6040, Mission Viejo, CA 92690

Bird Guides

Peterson, Roger Tory. 1980. *A Field Guide to the Birds*. Boston: Houghton Mifflin.

Peterson, Roger Tory. 1972. *A Field Guide to Western Birds*. Boston: Houghton Mifflin.

Scott, Shirley L., ed. 1983. *Field Guide to the Birds of North America*. Washington, DC: National Geographic Society.

Stokes, Donald W., and Lillian Q. Stokes. 1979. *A Guide to Bird Behavior*. Vol. 1. Boston: Little, Brown.

Stokes, Donald W., and Lillian Q. Stokes. 1983. *A Guide To Bird Behavior*. Vol. 2. Boston: Little, Brown.

Stokes, Donald W., and Lillian Q. Stokes. 1989. *A Guide To Bird Behavior*. Vol. 3. Boston: Little, Brown.

Wildflower Mixes

Clyde Robin Seed Company, 25670 Nickel Place, Hayward, CA 94545

Pennington Enterprises, P.O. Box 290, Madison, GA 30650

White Swan Ltd., 8104 SW Nimbis Ave., Beaverton, OR 97005

Manufacturers of Hummingbird Feeders

Aspects, Inc., 245 Child St., P.O. Box 408, Warren, RI 02885

Briggs Associates, Inc., 851-A4 Highway 224, Denver, CO 80229

Droll Yankees, Inc., 27 Mill Rd., Foster, RI 02825

Heath Manufacturing Co., 140 Mill St., Coopersville, MI 49404

Hyde Bird Feeder Company, P.O. Box 168, Waltham, MA 02254

North States Industries, Inc., 1200 Mendelssohn Ave., Suite 210, Minneapolis, MN 55427

Opus, P.O. Box 525, Bellingham, MA 02019

Penn Pak, Inc., P.O. Box 290, Madison, GA 30650

Perky-Pet Products, Inc., 2201 South Wabash, Denver, CO 80231

Presto Galaxy, Inc., 255 Banker St., Greenpoint, NY 11222

Rubbermaid, Inc., 1147 Akron Rd., Wooster, OH 44691

Woodsworld Hummingbird Society, 218 Buena Vista Ave., Santa Cruz, CA 95062

Retail Mail-Order Catalogs Specializing in Bird Products

Audubon Park Company, Drawer W., Akron, CO, 80720

Audubon Workshop, Inc., 1501 Paddock Dr., Northbrook, IL 60062

Barn Owl Gift Shop, 2509 Lakeshore Dr., Fennville, MI 49408

The Brown Company, P.O. Box 277, Yagoo Pond Rd., West Kingston, RI 02892

The Crow's Nest Bookshop, Laboratory of Ornithology at Cornell University, 159 Sapsucker Woods Rd., Ithaca, NY 14850

Duncraft, 33 Fisherville Rd., Penacook, NH 03303

Hyde Bird Feeder Company, 56 Felton St., P.O. Box 168, Waltham, MA 02254

Old Elm Feed and Supplies, P.O. Box 825, 13400 Watertown Plank Rd., Elm Grove, WI 53122

Ol' Sam Peabody Company, P.O. Box 316, Berrien Springs, MI 49103

Wild Bird Supplies, 4815 Oak St., Crystal Lake, IL 60012

The Wood Thrush Shop, 992 Davidson Dr., Nashville, TN 37205

Hummingbirds at a feeder by Penn Pak, Inc.